# OUTLAW

## THE TRUE STORY OF

## CLAUDE

## DALLAS

# OUTLAW

## THE TRUE STORY OF
## *CLAUDE*
## *DALLAS*
### BY JEFF LONG

*William Morrow and Company, Inc.* · *New York*

Library of Congress Cataloging in Publication Data

Long, Jeff.
Outlaw : the saga of Claude Dallas.

1. Dallas, Claude.   2. Crime and criminals—Idaho—
Biography.   3. Murder—Idaho—Case studies.   4. Trials
(Murder)—Idaho—case studies.   I. Title.
HV6248.D225L66   1985      364.1′523′0924 [B]    84-1178
ISBN 0-688-04165-5

Printed in the United States of America

First Edition

1 2 3 4 5 6 7 8 9 10

BOOK DESIGN BY LINEY LI

*To my mother and my father*

# *Acknowledgments*

**W**HILE this story largely spoke itself, there were those who helped enunciate its rhythms and decode its subtler shades. I am most indebted to John Accola of the *Idaho Statesman* for his advice, support, and three years of hospitality; to Cindy Butler for her fine research; and to the members of the Paradise Valley Folklife Project (1978–1982), of the American Folk-life Center at the Library of Congress, particularly Carl Fleischhauer, for their sensitive care of that endangered species known as oral history. Thanks also to Gary Strauss, David Brookman, and John Blackmer, all of the *Idaho Statesman;* to Wayne Cornell of the *Idaho Press Tribune;* to John Kennedy, formerly with the Associated Press; to Rex Bovee of the *Hum-*

*boldt Sun;* to Vincent Virga and Greg Claitor; and to James Miller and Ilene Stambaugh at Mount Gilead High School. I owe special thanks to my agent, Gwen Edelman, for help above and beyond the call, and to Diane for her encouragement and patience.

# OUTLAW

## THE TRUE STORY OF
## CLAUDE
## DALLAS

. . . driven to bay, he turns fiercely on his persecutors and makes a desperate effort to chase the whole pack of them from the land, to clear the air of their swarming multitudes, that he may breathe more freely and go on his way unmolested, at least for a time . . . They think that if they can only shake off these, their accursed tormentors, they will make a fresh start in life, happy and innocent; the tales of Eden and the old poetic age will come true again.

—From *The Golden Bough: The Scapegoat*,
SIR JAMES GEORGE FRAZER

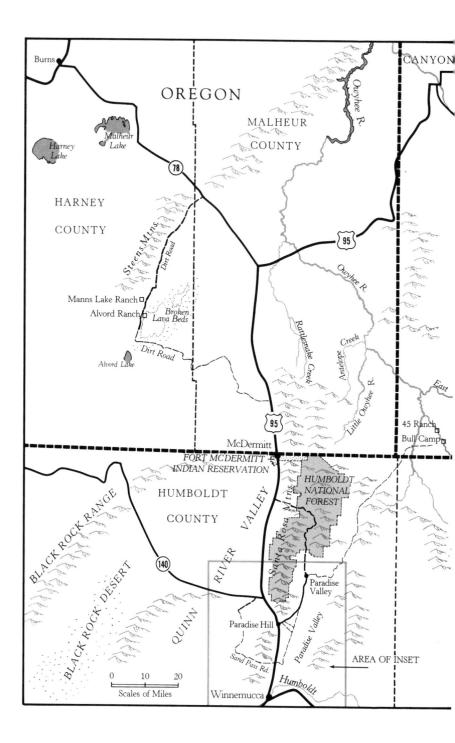

Burns

OREGON

MALHEUR
COUNTY

Ouyhee R.

CANYON

Harney
Lake

Malheur
Lake

78

HARNEY

COUNTY

Steens Mtns.

Dirt Road

Manns Lake Ranch

Alvord Ranch

Broken
Lava Beds

Dirt Road

Alvord Lake

95

Ouyhee R.

Rattlesnake Creek

Antelope

Creek

Little Ouyhee R.

East

45 Ranch
Bull Camp

95

McDermitt

FORT MCDERMITT
INDIAN RESERVATION

HUMBOLDT
NATIONAL
FOREST

BLACK ROCK RANGE

HUMBOLDT

COUNTY

RIVER VALLEY

Santa Rosa Mtns.

140

BLACK ROCK DESERT

QUINN

Paradise Hill

Sand Pass Rd.

Winnemucca

Humboldt

Paradise
Valley

Paradise Valley

AREA OF INSET

0      10      20
Scales of Miles

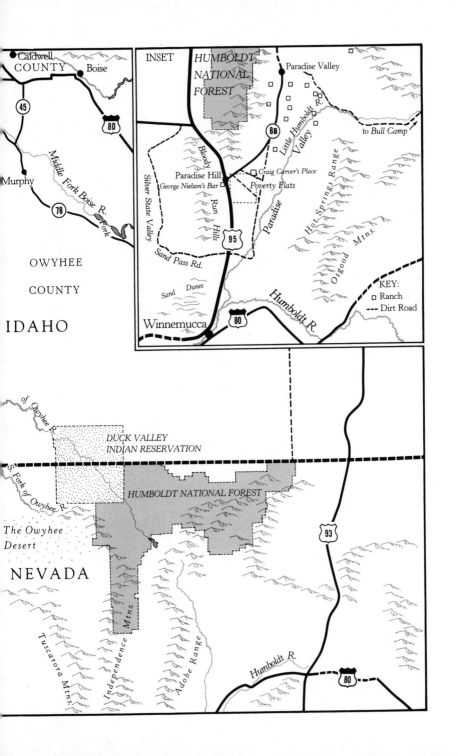

# Chapter 1

**J**UST north of the Nevada border between the Fort McDermitt Indian Reservation in Oregon and the Duck Valley Indian Reservation in Idaho, at the pit of a remote, labyrinthine canyon gashed deep by the South Fork of the Owyhee River, is a basin known as Bull Camp. Half lost to our century, it sits like an island beneath a rolling, high-altitude plateau that is full-blown American desert, arid, empty-looking country where nothing stands higher than sagebrush. The whole region bears the name Owyhee for three Hawaiian trapper-explorers who departed from the main body of Donald McKenzie's fur-trapping expedition in 1819 and vanished forever. They were not the last to be swallowed whole.

The spirit of the land is illusion . . . hills yield to similar hills, canyons lead to other canyons, the sky haunts, there are colors with no name, circles with no end . . . and that breeds a special kind of faith. Faith populated the territory after a little pioneer girl collected some pretty, yellow nuggets in her blue bucket during a wagon train's rest stop, but would never remember where precisely. Faith, bolstered by 16-shot Henry rifles and cavalry-issued Springfields addressed the savagery of Bannock Indians and renegade whites. Faith stole. Faith murdered. Faith preserved. It eased the pain of the massacres, the husbands who never reached home, the sisters and wives found mutilated; for a period of years, not a single person in the Owyhee region died except violently. The quartz ledges quit giving gold; the lush bunchgrass plains were ravaged by short-sighted cattle barons and turned to cheatgrass and sagebrush; there were false starts and hard times and funerals without bodies. But those who believed in the land took the realities with the illusions. And those who believed in it became part of it, the land, the illusion. The irony is that so many calloused, sunburned realists could believe so much in so little, over and over. Such is the nature of frontiers.

Through that echoing territory where the water hides in deep mazes from the sun, Claude Dallas arrived at Bull Camp in the spring of 1980. He beached his canoe, built a fire, and spent the night by a roofless, collapsing stone hut where the river takes its slow bend. Hugged tight by basalt walls, the world was narrow and private, and there has always been something truer about the beauty when you've bought it with your muscles and sweat. The seduction went something like this: lying there with the Milky Way bracketed by two high walls, he smelled the sage and listened to the passing water. With an easy heart, he recognized which sounds belonged to what animal. Except for the skeletal stone hut, a remnant of the mining days when oxen were rotated up from Nevada mines for rest, Bull Camp was vital and animate. Spring was on and game was abundant. The isolation was like a song. That night he promised himself to return here and winter, alone, the way he liked to be. By noon the next day, Bull Camp was empty.

Twelve years earlier he had entered the high desert, eighteen years old and as shy as he was green, holding close to him the myths of the raw West. Square-built like a wrestler, he was fit and strong and could walk forty miles in a day. One morning he'd simply appeared in Paradise Hill, Nevada, along Highway 95, riding a buckskin, packing another, and toting a rifle, bent on a different era. No one knew quite where he had come from, back east somewhere, and no one particularly cared. He was a hard, intelligent worker and, after some years, a good cowboy. From his first year buckarooing for the Quarter Circle A outfit, the year he hand-filed a pair of spurs and made his own "woollies," a local chaps to protect against thorns and barbwire, he had done some growing. By the age of thirty his beard had grown full, giving him a different sort of handsomeness. And after one particularly harrowing winter alone in the desert ("Nothing but straight horsemeat for two months, mustang, because I was afoot and couldn't get meat"), he kept his brown hair long and tied in a ponytail. Except for wire-rimmed glasses that lent a donnish touch, he looked like his beloved mountain men, a parallel so uncanny that more than one rancher had trouble believing his name wasn't a fiction. Claude Dallas took the style to heart.

Before the year was out he was back at Bull Camp, fixed to run his seventy-trap line and spend some solitary time. His move to the basin in early December was a companionable occasion with eight friends . . . among them Jim Stevens, George Nielsen, and Craig Carver . . . and a miniature caravan comprising an old bus, a Chevy Suburban to pull the horse-trailer, and a pickup truck. It was a hundred-mile journey to the rim overlooking Bull Camp, six slow hours along a trail finally devoured by sagebrush. The landmarks are subtle . . . a broken windmill, a shapeless butte, an unmarked junction of nonexistent roads. It is a strange wilderness that reads as if it were tamed. Tiny, inquisitive clusters of cattle meander on the dusty terrain, here and there a water tank festers, and barbwire chases infinity. The mountains are unspectacular, more flat than bold, and everything seems straightforward. The rolling flatness deceives. Either you know the terrain or it puts you in circles.

They left Dallas at the rim with several hundred pounds of trapsets, gear, kerosene, food, and guns, and two mules rented from a rancher. "The wind was ablowin', and it was snowin' like the devil," said Frank Gavica, one of the caravan members. "It just made me feel bad. That's dangerous out there, ten miles from hell and a thousand from anyplace else, all by yourself down by the crick. What would happen if you got hurt? If there was two men . . . but only one man like that? No. I asked him, 'Why do you do it?' And he said, 'It's my life.'" During the next few weeks he humped loads down the steep trail from the rim and set up camp across the river from the crumbling land-mark building, erecting a large white canvas tent with a wood-burning stove inside, and setting the mules loose on rock drags when he wasn't riding or packing them. Some deer drifted into the area before Christmas, and though the season was long since over and he knew it, Dallas "knocked down" two bucks and a dry doe. Dressing the carcasses, he hung the quarters in the stone hut under a plastic tarp, but later moved the meat into camp and hung it from his steel tent poles. From these he periodically carved steaks and, as the trapline took shape, used pieces to bait his sets with exposed venison, which was illegal. He caught and skinned a couple of bobcats. Again he knew it was illegal.

Then on New Year's Eve, trouble arrived on horseback in the person of Eddie Carlin, a trapper and caretaker at the nearby 45 Ranch. Carlin forded the river and Dallas boiled water over a campfire to make his guest tea. It was not their first confrontation and the conversation was chilly. It was clear that Carlin viewed Dallas as an interloper. First he accused Dallas of disturbing the 45's cattle, but Dallas knew that Carlin knew that was a lie. The cows were enjoying a warm winter on the plateau, and not one had descended below a drift fence one hundred feet under the rim. "When he tried to put that on me, I told him I knew better," Dallas said. "We got that straightened out." Carlin was jumpy, alarmed by a .357 Magnum on the trapper's right hip. The talk turned to the real issue, territory. "Ed implied that was their country. I told him I'd looked for signs of trappers and hadn't found any old sets." Dallas wasn't about to budge. He knew that, like most of Owyhee County, this was Bureau of Land Management (BLM) land, public property. All the same, he agreed to stay south of Coyote Hole. Then Carlin had the bad taste to remark on the cat pelts airing in camp and the poached venison. Again Dallas didn't budge. He joked about the pelts. "Those cats don't know it's not the ninth [of January, the first day of bobcat season]." And of the deer quarters, he announced, "A man's got to eat. I don't try to hide my meat when I'm in this kind of country. You've got two things to eat, you either eat venison or you eat beef. And I've never killed another man's beef." Every time Dallas stood up, Carlin stood up, plainly discomposed. The caretaker had come to clear the basin. Instead, Dallas had buffaloed him. It was that gun. Trying to reconstruct at least the appearance of prerogative, Carlin artlessly mentioned that he and his father, Don, had turned people in to the Fish and Game Department before. Of course, he added, they wouldn't turn Dallas in, the Carlins weren't like that. Dallas changed the subject and mentioned how this was his final season in Nevada, he was going to Alaska in June. After an hour, the two men finished their tea and sparring, and Carlin mounted up. Just as he left Bull Camp, he promised once again not to blow the whistle, but warned that Fish and Game might just show up anyway.

Prophetically, Dallas replied, "I'll be ready for them."

A few days later two ex-government trappers from Oregon nested on 45 property and the Carlins panicked. Suddenly perceiving themselves to be overwhelmed on a finite plot they regarded as their own, the Carlins did what they'd done before. A year earlier Don Carlin had been fined for illegally baiting his traps. Now, on Sunday, January 4, the elder Carlin called one of the same men who had caught him, Idaho Fish and Game Warden Bill Pogue, and declared that trappers were poaching in the area and baiting their traps with sage hens. Although the violations were misdemeanors, the distance from backup put Pogue on the alert.

Bill Pogue was known among his fellow officers as a lawman's lawman, a good, tough officer. There was no nonsense about the fifty-year-old man, and he was not famous for compromise. To Pogue the law was the law. That inflexibility was not designed to earn him popularity, just obedience, and there were stories about his manner. "He had more badge than he could stand," one hunter would describe him. Even his close friends remarked on his demeanor: "When Bill walked up to you, there was no question in your mind that he represented the law." Pogue had a stare, a blind, cold eye caused by a camping accident, which locked his presence in. "People remembered that he'd looked at them," said a friend. "There wasn't any way you were going to forget the man."

The area in which the complaint had been lodged was not Pogue's district, but his deep affection for the Owyhee region made him decide to investigate the violations himself. He telephoned Michael Elms, the officer in charge of the area, but Elms was sick. Pogue then called a second warden, also indisposed, and finally found a partner in Wilson Conley Elms, Michael Elms's younger brother. Conley Elms was a huge, gentle man with a passion for fly-fishing and a reputation for dependability.

Shortly before midnight the two men set out from Boise for the 45 Ranch, four hours away. They slept for two or three hours in the bed of their pickup truck, then at dawn descended a steep dirt road to the ranch. Over breakfast, Carlin described the location of the two Oregonian trappers to the wardens. As they prepared to leave with a thermos of hot coffee in hand and an invitation to supper with the Carlins, the wardens asked if there were any other trappers in the area. Ed Carlin didn't answer, but his wife did. "What about that man up the canyon—Dallas?" she threw in. "Dallas," Pogue repeated. He seemed to recognize the name. They'd never met, but a year earlier Pogue had entered Dallas's vacant winter campsite in Star Valley and introduced himself with a terse note on the back of his calling card. "I'll check on you later," it had said. "William H. Pogue." He left no question in your mind, he represented the law.

Now that Dallas had been mentioned, Ed Carlin amplified on the lone trapper. He told about the meat and fur and cautioned against turning one's back on the man. Pogue nodded. ("Bill never sat with his back to the door or windows," it would be recalled.) Carlin warned the wardens that Dallas always carried a .357 Magnum on his right hip. "All right," Pogue plotted out loud to his partner. "We'll keep each other covered." Crossing the river in their pickup, the wardens contacted the two trappers from Oregon and cited them for illegal baiting and trapping out of season. "You either sign these tickets or you go to jail," Pogue told them gruffly. "You make up your minds which way you want to go." Around noon the lawmen drove on along the west rim of the deep canyon in search of Claude Dallas.

Dallas needed a storm. The winter had been unseasonably warm, with no more than "one little skiff of snow" since he'd moved into camp. Already the warm spell had ended any worthwhile coyote take; they had been "rubbing" for over a month, which broke the hair and gave their fur a singed look, putting them past prime. Normally in that high, cold desert country, the bobcats stay prime as late as March, but Dallas had begun to resign himself to a short season. This morning, however, the sky showed signs of a coming storm and that put him in good spirits because just before and right after a storm, he had noticed "the cats really seem to move."

He was dressed in Levi's, an uncreased, wide-brim cowboy hat, and a yellow fireman's turnout jacket for a windbreaker as he bucked up a pile of sagebrush for firewood and grained the mules. He left camp late, ice still glazing the river rock, around 8:30. Climbing out across the basin, he was checking and remaking sprung traps when he thought he heard a gunshot from the west rim where the camp trail originated. That was only part of a prearranged signal that someone had arrived on the rim and was descending with groceries, mail, and supplies, and he was unsure, thinking it might have been chukar hunters. All the same, Dallas fired his own gun once in return, and started the long climb up the trail. He was expecting George Nielsen, a crusty, aging roadside bar owner and friend of a dozen years.

Instead, not far below the rim's ridge, he found another friend, Jim Stevens. A potato farmer from the dusty croplands between Paradise Valley and Winnemucca, Stevens had met the trapper four years earlier while working on a grain combining crew for which Dallas drove truck. When Dallas reached him on the trail, Stevens was carrying a shotgun rolled in his sleeping bag and a Styrofoam cooler. Something of a history buff, he was fascinated by his friend's robust fidelity to an obscure craft. Once he had spent a dawn-to-dusk day walking a trapline with Dallas in the Bloody Run Hills near Paradise Hill. Another time he had loaned the man his antique .50 caliber Hawkins, the buffalo gun preferred by early mountain men, and when it was returned the rifle was oiled and in better condition than he'd ever seen it. In addition to sharing camp with the trapper, Stevens had seen some old wagon wheels on his first trip in December and was hoping to unearth a few pioneer artifacts or arrowheads. He had even brought in a metal detector and shovel.

They were happy to see each other. The morning's rim fog had burned away, leaving the canyon sharp and lovely. The first thing Dallas asked for was fruit; he'd been eating nothing but venison for more than a week. There was not only fruit, but pistachio pudding and brownies Stevens's wife had made. "We're going to have a good time," Dallas predicted. There were more supplies in Stevens's Blazer, and rather than go all the way down to fetch the mules, Dallas decided to pack down what he could on foot. Stevens continued down to the river camp. The trail had started to thaw and was a little greasy. Just as the trapper topped the rim, he saw two men approaching.

They were government, he discerned, and had a good notion what kind of government because they had patches on their shoulders and had driven a Fish and Game truck. "One of them was a big man," Dallas understated of Conley Elms, who was over six feet tall and weighed upward of 280 pounds. The other man, "Well, he wasn't all that small." Also, Dallas noticed, the older, smaller man was wearing a hip gun. Well versed in weaponry, himself the owner of a fair-sized arsenal, Dallas immediately recognized the make, a standard law issue, four-inch Smith and Wesson. He never quit noticing Pogue's gun.

Dallas was carrying two revolvers himself, that .357 Magnum on his hip which had put Ed Carlin on edge, plus a .22 Smith and Wesson in a shoulder holster. The .22 was his trap gun. There are two common methods of finishing off game in a trap. One is to stun the animal with a blow to the snout, then upend it and crush the rib cage with your boot. The quicker but bloodier method is to shoot the animal in the head with a small caliber bullet.

Pogue did the talking for himself and Elms, first declaring they were Fish and Game, then their names. No hands were shaken. There were rumors of meat and cats down in Bull Camp, Pogue brusquely stated, and he had come to check on them. It was two months too late to be shooting deer legally, and four days too early to be trapping bobcats. Dallas was unabashed. "I have some meat hung up," he confirmed. "I have to eat." The wardens were welcome to his camp, he said.

Dallas had a way of talking about his camp which instantly informed you that here was domain. He worked hard at keeping a clean, neat site, and took pride in its simplicity and order. If a man came into his camp, Dallas liked him to understand whose camp it was. But Pogue wasn't the kind of man to entertain illusions. He was here for law, not coffee. This was his territory, those deer and cats were under his protection. He didn't need an invitation to enter anybody's camp, or a search warrant to enter their tent.

"If you guys came out here a hundred and fifty miles just to give me a citation for meat," the long-haired trapper challenged, "I can't see it."

Pogue got mad. "He flew hot," Dallas said. "He seemed to be on the fight. He read me the riot act right there. You know, he started off, he said, 'I'm going to tell you something right now, Dallas, if you want to get along with me.'"

And again Dallas noticed Pogue's gun.

Every time Dallas moved or spoke, Pogue's hand seemed to move toward the law issue gun on his hip. After fifteen minutes of confrontation, the trapper trying to bluff his way clear, the warden obviously fed up, Dallas finally resigned himself to the fact that they were going down into his camp. He had come all this way up to the rim, though, and was not about to waste a trip. He started for the Blazer to load his pack full. Immediately the two wardens separated and flanked him. "They acted as if I had just robbed a bank." Pogue's gun was already "clear," in the holster but with the security strap unsnapped. Now Dallas saw Elms reach inside his unzipped jacket and apparently free a gun, too, this one in a shoulder rig. Small details registered, facts that would have escaped other people. The safety strap on Pogue's holster, for what it mattered, was not a thumb break.

Dallas knew his firearms. He was a crack shot and a quick-draw artist and had studied police and military training manuals on combat shooting. Preparation was an ethic, central to his Spartan existence. He had spent that bad winter eating mustangs because he had gone in without mules, and the lesson had been learned: Be ready. Readiness was survival.

And he was ready to survive in every way he could. His .357 Magnum had customized wooden stocks, and he carried two speed loaders for it, the same number as for several of his other handguns. Farmers above Winnemucca had even seen him pack a handgun while driving a tractor or when welding. Dallas made no bones about it. "I've had some scrapes where I didn't have my handgun, and I'd like to have had one. I've been hung up several times alone and taken some bad falls. I had to cut myself away from a horse once. If I'm ever out away from camp and break a leg, I sure as hell want to have a gun with me."

As Dallas finished loading supplies in his pack, Pogue returned to the Fish and Game truck and conspicuously removed a pair of handcuffs along with a small canvas backpack. Dallas had an opinion about each. The backpack he silently disparaged as cheap, "one of those little Boy Scout jobs." As for the handcuffs, they weren't necessary. Dallas let Pogue know that he thought the treatment was "a little bit out of line." Predictably by now, that "fired the man off" again. An inevitability had begun to settle over the pocket of men.

"You can go easy or you can go hard," Pogue replied. "It doesn't make any difference to me." You make up your mind which way you want to go, he had told the two trappers from Oregon. Easy or hard, it would echo in Dallas's mind and justify much to him. "Let's go," Pogue directed.

The three men started down the trail, passing through a gate in the cattle drift fence below the rim. Elms walked behind the trapper, Pogue flanked him off the trail to one side. Halfway down the gorge, Dallas stopped to rest and there was that image again, Pogue's hand on the butt of his gun. "You'll find traveling a lot easier on the trail," Dallas commented to the warden. Their animosity had reached the proportions of a dance, one man cueing the other's belligerence, both of them hostile. Pogue snapped back that he could take care of himself. Still flanked, Dallas continued down to the canyon floor.

Unaware of the wardens, Jim Stevens had descended to Bull Camp, doffed his load, and sauntered upriver. Already he had turned up an arrowhead and was looking for more. Dallas hollered that they had company and headed toward his tent with the pack full of groceries. Pogue stopped him short. It was time to disarm the trapper.

Most men whom wardens contact in the field carry guns and knives. Few welcome the idea of the law poking through their campsites. Pogue had seen a bulge in the left armpit of Dallas's windbreaker and wanted that gun, butt first, no fast moves. Dallas considered it unusual that he should be disarmed, but surrendered it all the same . . . his .22 trap gun. Pogue unloaded the .22 revolver and put it into his jacket pocket. Incredibly he didn't notice the gun on the trapper's hip which Carlin had warned him about, nor did Dallas volunteer its presence. He had been arrested seven years earlier for draft evasion, and had been raised by a father with a distaste for the law. Standard procedure offended his sensibilities. The .357 Magnum stayed in its holster, a bullet in the chamber. That was the way he kept all his guns, ready.

Dallas was feeling molested. They were one hundred miles into the past and this was his camp. He had made it not only with his hands, but with his life. He had spent twelve years paying dues in this country, buckarooing "on the mountain" (a cattlemen's term connoting almost anywhere on the high Sonoran range used for summer grazing), and harvesting and digging wells. He had wintered alone many times, endured, fashioned a style. This camp was an expression of something he had decided on a long time ago. "You are welcome in my camp," he once told a Nevada game warden, "but leave your badge outside." When the warden explained that that was impossible, Dallas had answered, "Don't come into my camp then." Now there was a badge in his camp, and this surly lawman had just taken one of his guns.

They met Jim Stevens at the tent. The first thing Pogue did was strip him, too, of his gun. Stevens was wearing a .357 Magnum on his belt. George Nielsen had given it to him at dawn in Paradise Hill to signal with. Shucking the bullets into his hand, Pogue then handed the revolver back and put the cartridges in Stevens's jacket pocket. The potato farmer was obliging and Pogue's temper began to cool, though not for long. Venison was airing on the tent poles, and while Dallas thought an explanation was enough, Pogue didn't. He'd caught arrogance red-handed, an all-too-rare occasion. The trapper produced his Idaho and Nevada hunting and trapping licenses. Pogue checked them. They went back and forth about the meat for another five minutes, "and Pogue was getting hot again."

Dallas knew he'd violated the letter of the law, but for him it was the spirit of the law that was paramount. That the deer season was closed did not mean he couldn't kill deer, because the "season" was for other men. "Not anyone else that I know lives like I do or under the conditions that I do," he would say. When it came from a lawman's mouth, "season" was a limiting term, and Dallas was beyond limits. When Ed Carlin had reminded him that the bobcat season was still two weeks away, Dallas had shrugged. His relationship was to nature, not the law, to the seasons, not the "season." Over the years, to various people, he had evoked the ambiguous, informal "subsistence law" which holds that a man should be able to take an animal when he is hungry. Besides, he argued, "It's not practical to carry in the kind of meat you need to carry you through the winter. You can't bring in cut meat and frozen meat. Meat has to be hung in carcass form to keep. I could have made arrangements, but even if I'd have wanted to, I couldn't have afforded it. It's unreasonable," he concluded, "to give me a citation living this remote and under these conditions."

Pogue was unimpressed. Idaho Fish and Game arrests twenty-five to thirty trappers and prosecutes some two to three thousand other violations every year. Dallas was just one more. The only principle at stake here was law, and this long-haired, contrary trapper had clearly broken it.

Down for fun, not trouble, Stevens grew embarrassed for his friend and drifted away from the conversation. He turned his back on the party and faced the river. While he stared off across the water, the wrangling went on, the tone civil but unfriendly. Pogue said he was going to search the tent. Dallas demanded his search warrant. "That tent is my home," he said. "If you can't produce a search warrant I don't want you in my tent."

Pogue didn't have one or need one. "You can go easy or you can go hard, Dallas," he said. "It doesn't make any difference to me." And Dallas saw the image yet again, the warden's hand on the butt of his gun, "like he was itching to use it." The game warden's voice was louder now. "Strict," said Stevens, "like a drill instructor."

"Do you want to get the cats," Pogue demanded, "or do I have to get them?" He motioned his gigantic partner to search the tent. Elms moved forward, untied the flap, and entered. The cat pelts were on the back wall. "There's a coon in here, too," he called from the inside. A raccoon had gotten in a trap and now it was drying on a stretcher board. A moment later Elms reappeared carrying the bobcat hides, which he placed on the ground in front of the tent.

"We're going to confiscate those cats, Dallas," Pogue said.

"Now wait a minute," Dallas argued. "You don't know that I didn't get those pelts in Nevada." The Nevada line was four miles south, and in that state the bobcat season had ended just five days before. "I showed you my license. I have a residence license in Nevada. I have a nonresident in Idaho. I'm running traplines here with some mules. I'm not even sure where the state line is."

Pogue insisted the pelts were illegal. Technically they were, even if they'd come from Nevada during the Nevada season, because they had to be tagged before being moved across the border. Dallas protested. With no transportation but mules, how could he have taken the pelts in for tagging? In lieu of that, he argued, was he supposed to "leave the pelts hang on a bush down there?" The violations were nonextraditable offenses, misdemeanors usually cited with a ticket. Trying to salvage what he could from the worsening situation, Dallas asked if Pogue would simply cite him for the venison. But the trapper had already indicated his opinion of the legal system, and Pogue decided Dallas would never show up in court. No, he said, he was going to seize the pelts, arrest Dallas, and take him in. It was Pogue's ace in the hole, his spoiler. Both men knew what an arrest would mean. By the time Dallas could raise bail and somehow make his way back from Boise to Bull Camp, the camp would fall apart, his mules would stray, his trapline would degenerate, his hard work would be ruined. A second time Dallas asked just to be cited. Not three hours earlier, Pogue had caught two other nonresident trappers and simply cited them. It was entirely his choice. He'd already chosen.

"You can go easy or you can go hard," came the echo.

Dallas protested. "I've got my livestock, my mules here, and I've got all my equipment here. I can't leave them."

"You can go hard," Pogue warned. "I can carry you out."

"You're out of your mind," Dallas pitched back. "You can't shoot a man over a game violation."

"I'll carry you out," Pogue said.

In the following instant, the dream of the old West, the legends and machismo and mean truths caught them tight. "Hard," said Dallas. "That's only one way. That's dead."

"I can carry you out." Dallas was sure he saw Pogue reach for his gun.

Still gazing at the river, Stevens heard Pogue shout, "Oh no." Simultaneously gunfire thundered in a deafening volley. Shocked, Stevens wheeled and saw smoke pouring from Bill Pogue's chest even as the man was backing up and falling down. Dallas was in a low crouch. In the span of five seconds, he fired his first two rounds into Pogue, saw Elms reaching for a gun, shot him once, saw Pogue bringing his gun to bear, shot twice, then "threw" the last bullet at Elms.

Horrified, Stevens watched Dallas dash into his tent and grab a lever action .22 rifle, another of his trap guns. Elms was face down and Pogue was on his back. Pogue lifted his head, then laid it back down. Dallas emerged. Quickly, without hesitation, he placed one shot into each man's head, trapper style. Beyond any question now, they were dead.

For a minute he just stood there, rifle in hand, trying to compose himself. Slowly he returned to the deep canyon and the present. He noticed that his friend had run forty yards upriver. Stevens was terrified, sure Dallas was going to kill him too. Even so, he turned around and slowly walked back to the tent. "Why, Claude?" he asked. "Why?"

"I swore I'd never be arrested again," Dallas answered. "They had handcuffs on. I'm sorry to get you involved." Then he added, "I've got to get rid of the bodies."

"I'll help you, Claude," Stevens said. He was almost delirious with horror. Minutes before, he'd been gazing at the river,
thinking of arrowheads. Now two bodies lay at his feet with
holes in their skulls. The canyon with its high walls suddenly
had the look of the world's far edge.

It was still early afternoon. Dallas was afraid that a BLM
plane might suddenly appear over the corner of the rim and
spot the bodies. He had no delusions about whom he'd killed.
They were lawmen. He'd killed two cops. Speaking faster than
normal, his plans shaping by the instant, Dallas directed Stevens to cover the two wardens with the sagebrush he had cut
earlier for firewood, and then forded the river to fetch the
larger mule. His instinct was to erase everything: the bodies,
the evidence, the crime, even the criminal. Each cascading
thought over the next hours built toward that erasure, even
though it was impossible. The futility of undoing his deed expressed itself repeatedly, but Dallas never quit trying. To start
with, the mules had been spooked by the gunfire and were
skittish, and even though it was on a rock drag, the larger mule
could not be caught.

While the trapper was trying to catch a mule across the
river, Stevens covered the bodies where they lay with fur
stretching boards and brushwood. Perceptions were arriving in
more even blocks now. He had seen smoke enveloping Pogue's
chest, had watched Elms stumble and land on his face, had
heard the rifle shots into each skull, but would not recall running upriver from the scene or his shaking return. He saw
Pogue's service revolver several inches from his outstretched
hand as he covered the body. Then he sat down on a rock to
compose himself. There was no reason to believe Dallas was
going to spare his life, he thought. The shooting made no
sense, Dallas made no sense, why should the friendship make

sense? All that made sense was that the sole eyewitness would have to disappear also. Stevens looked across the river at Dallas and reloaded his gun which Pogue had emptied. But he couldn't shoot a friend, and so he put the gun away. Nor did he run away. There was no place to run to. He would have been an open target for a full half hour while climbing back up to the rim, and he had a heart condition to boot. Instead, when the trapper called over to get a pan of grain for the smaller mule, Stevens obeyed. His nerves were so frayed that he spilled grain all over the tent floor.

With the pan of grain, Dallas finally managed to catch the little jenny. He led her to camp, saddled her with a sawbuck for load carrying, hobbled her "fore and aft," then tied the hobbles together. The brush and stretcher boards were pulled off, and the two men set to loading on a body. The first was Pogue's, but not before Dallas removed all the personal effects from the clothing and pockets and put them in Pogue's canvas backpack. "This gun," he said, picking up Pogue's revolver, "is going into the ground with this guy." And plucking off the warden's sixteen-year service badge, he said, "It's hard to believe anybody could work for Fish and Game for that long."

Then they loaded Pogue's body onto the mule. "If they'd taken me on the rim," Dallas commented aloud, "they'd have killed me." He lashed Pogue tight to the sawbuck and started up, moving fast even though he was carrying the same backpack full of groceries he had descended with not long before. At the trapper's command, Stevens started up the trail, too, carrying his shotgun, sleeping bag, and the Styrofoam cooler. He was still ascending when Dallas met him returning for a second load. Stevens placed his possessions on the trail and followed the trapper and mule back to camp.

"They had no business in my camp," Dallas said as they

started to work with the second body. He was optimistic. "I may not get caught for seven or eight years, and maybe when I do, I'll only get seven or eight years." Elms's body was very bloody and the ground beneath was stained. "If you're going to throw up," Dallas told the farmer, "go off into the brush there." Unable to lift the heavy body, they dragged it close to the river and led the mule down a depression beside it. From there they were able to roll the body onto the wooden packsaddle. This time Stevens was detailed to lead the mule up. Soon, looking down from the trail, he saw huge clouds of smoke rising from camp and figured Dallas was burning the whole camp to the ground. In fact, he had only set fire to two piles of wood, one for each body, in an attempt to scorch clean the bloodstained earth. All evidence that two wardens had visited his camp was nearly gone. The revolvers, service badges, and pocket effects were safely in Pogue's daypack. The bloodstains were being incinerated. One body was up. The other was on its way. He was thinking clearly and well, the erasure was working. And then the mule fell over.

She weighed no more than five hundred pounds, and there was half that much in muscle and blood on her back. Halfway up the trail, on the first bench, the body shifted and the jenny fell over. The cinched ropes tightened around her chest, her head fell back and her eyes closed. She was suffocating. Without a second thought, Stevens untied the ropes. The mule stood up with the load between her legs. Dallas arrived.

For the next forty-five minutes, the two men tried to lift the huge, bloody body back onto the mule. They tried everything, and in the process ripped off the warden's shirt and undershirt, then broke off his belt buckle, and ended up cutting his pants free with a sheath knife. They kept trying to dress the body, but the pants always ended up at his ankles.

"The only way to get him up is to quarter him," Dallas finally offered in frustration.

"I don't have the stomach for that," Stevens answered back.

"There's no way I could do that either," Dallas agreed, and switched strategies. "I'm going to put him in the river. It's getting dark." Five hours had passed since the shooting. The winter sun was sinking. They tied a rope around the man's feet and knotted it to the mule, but all that accomplished was the removal of Elms's boots. They turned the body around and cinched the rope about his chest. As Dallas started the mule back down with the nude body, he instructed Stevens to smooth out the drag marks. The farmer started sweeping the earth with his feet until he was told, "Use your hands."

Once more Stevens moved upslope. Once more Dallas overtook him. It was dark now. The trapper was wearing Pogue's daypack filled with the warden's effects, on top of which he had tied two rifles and a shotgun, the bobcat hides, a burlap bag, and an orange tarp. The pack was so heavy a strap had broken and Dallas was holding it on with his hand. To this point he'd mentioned the shootings in terms of justified homicide, but now he had a darker opinion. "It's Murder One for me," he pronounced. "I didn't weight the body and they'll find it." That lessened his headstart, he felt, and that lessened his chances of survival. He had killed two cops.

Stevens was on the verge of collapse. "Set it down," Dallas said. "Take it easy. I don't want anything to happen to you. I don't want you to have a heart attack or anything." Stevens sat down, exhausted. Soon Dallas returned with a can of Seven-Up. Together they made it up to the Blazer.

Under the open tailgate lay Pogue's body, face up. Quickly now, they lifted the body onto the orange tarp in back of the Blazer, slid it in, and closed the tailgate. Pogue's legs had stiffened and they were forced to leave his ankles jutting through the rolled-up rear window. The night was cold. The windows had iced over. Stevens drove forward. Piling more stretcher boards and sagebrush over the ground on which Pogue's body had lain, Dallas poured on a can of kerosene and lit a match.

Hours later, they reached Paradise Hill, a dusty handful of trailers and one bar. It was nearly midnight. Dallas pounded at the door of his old friends George Nielsen, the bar owner, and his wife, Liz, the head nurse at Winnemucca's small hospital. Just that morning Nielsen had given Stevens the supplies and gun he had taken to Bull Camp. Now Dallas was standing in his doorway covered with blood.

"Two Fish and Game came into my camp," Dallas said. "I dusted them off. We have one out in the blue Blazer." He was wild-eyed. It was the Nielsens' turn to be frightened of the trapper, their turn to obey. All the bloody clothing had to be burned, he said. He needed to borrow Nielsen's pickup truck and some entrenching tools. Stevens should take a shower and be sure to wash under his fingernails. "Whatever you want, Claude," Liz Nielsen said. "We don't want any trouble."

Pogue's body was transferred from the Blazer to Nielsen's truck. The drama was winding to a close. Where he had been excited, now Dallas seemed sad. "Tell my parents I love them," he instructed Stevens. He loaded a shovel and grub hoe in the truck bed. At last he said good-bye to the farmer. "I'll probably never see you again."

By the time Dallas returned with the truck emptied two hours later, Stevens had slipped off to his family and farm down the road. Not much later, the bar owner claimed, Dallas rousted him from bed and asked to be driven to a point nearby on Sand Pass Road. In the truck Nielsen handed him a hundred dollars and a packet of beans and other food staples prepared by his wife. As they drove, Dallas said, "I did a sloppy job. But they deserved it, they had it coming." Then, in the early morning with the stars cutting sharp over the Bloody Run Hills, Nielsen watched Claude Dallas disappear into a patch of fog with a backpack, sleeping bag, duffel bag, rifle, and a heavy handgun. George Nielsen had been one of the first to meet Dallas when he arrived in Nevada eleven years earlier, a lone, dreaming teenager with two horses and a rifle, a boy tracking bygone times between the interstices of highways, barbwire, and law. Now he was the last to see him go.

# Chapter 2

IF only Jim Stevens could have slept that night, the legend might have died at the killing ground, far short of the ritual it became. If he could have slept, then maybe next morning or whenever they came for him, he could have lied and pronounced the alibi with conviction: *I was there. But earlier, before Claude ran amok. I don't know what happened. He asked for fruit. He read his mail. We talked. He seemed normal then. And then I drove back out from the desert.* With no witness to the event, Dallas might have sunk into the limbo of other desert wild men, the sort of dry wreckage they had all seen before. But as it was, the gentle farmer couldn't sleep that night, and by morning he couldn't lie. All night long he kept returning to the Owyhee.

   The long, dark, urgent ride out from Bull Camp became
for him a cold delirium of fear and exhaustion and deceptions.
As they drove off in his Blazer, he remembered, with the bright
kerosene fire of heaped stretcher boards and sagebrush marking the south rim of the gorge, Dallas suddenly spooked,
swearing he had spied headlights on the horizon. The light was
a trick, though, just a planet low among the stars. Dry brush
shrieked beneath their boots, clawing at the carriage and gas
tank. Near Greeley Crossing, a wash bracketed by two cattle
guards, they saw headlights again, and this time Dallas told the
farmer to let him out and continue driving. If this was the law,
he counseled Stevens, give them no cause to shoot, take no
chances. "Just put your hands up, just tell them I held a gun on
you and I'm out here in the sagebrush." Dallas slipped from the
Blazer and sank into the darkness. Stevens drove on. But again
it was an illusion. The lights belonged to a low-flying airplane.
Stevens could have sped off at that point, marooning Dallas
among the shadows and barbwire, but every time he looked in
the rearview mirror, there were the two feet of Bill Pogue
grimly sticking through the back window rolled as high as it
could go. The farmer was weary and in shock. He needed guid-
ance. Circling back, he shouted for Dallas. He heard a gunshot
and braked. From out of that warped, freezing night emerged
the trapper. Dallas climbed back in the passenger's door.
   It took them hours to exit the Owyhee, more than enough
time for Dallas to invent, discard, and reshape plausible alibis
for his dazed friend. They tried out the stories on each other. It
would be best, Dallas finally decided, if Stevens did not deny
that he'd been to Bull Camp. "You visited and delivered supplies, but you left. You saw nothing." Stevens demurred. The
alibi would erase any suspicions that he had aided in the murders. It would buy Stevens innocence. More important, and

this went unspoken, it would buy Dallas time. However briefly, the lie would bury details and impede what promised to be a massive manhunt. Dallas had no illusions about that.

"I don't know how you feel about it," Dallas probed as they drove on, "but I think it's justifiable homicide." His only answer was apprehensive silence. The trapper repeated his view. "You may feel different," he tried to persuade, "but I think it's justifiable homicide." Through it all, dread was as much a bond for Stevens as friendship. He had loaded his empty gun at Bull Camp and contemplated shooting the murderer, but they were friends. By not shooting Dallas, he'd proved it. The farmer had gambled that Dallas would reciprocate and prove the friendship and not shoot him down too. Each man doubted the other. Without a word about the dread, each maneuvered toward faith. When the body was mentioned, Stevens pointedly stated he didn't want to know where it would be buried. He dared not whisper his real reason for begging ignorance, that a grave can hold two bodies as easily as one.

At last they reached Paradise Valley, a shuttered-up ghost town but for some streetlamps, pickup trucks, and dogs, the cultural hub for ranches Dallas had cowboyed on. As they drove down its single paved lane with a dead man's feet jutting from the rear window, the town slept. Another eighteen miles through grazing range past wood signs announcing ranches up this or that dirt tributary, and they arrived at Paradise Hill, the tiny, low-rent colony built around George Nielsen's bar. Not yet twenty-four hours had passed since Stevens embarked from here into the fog of the Owyhee, bound for a bit of fishing and amateur archaeology at Bull Camp. Here he was back again. The body was transferred from his Blazer. Dallas said goodbye and departed with Nielsen's pickup. While he was gone, Stevens showered and changed into fresh clothes, careful to wash the blood from under his fingernails. When he entered the kitchen, Liz Nielsen was trying to stuff his bloody boots into the wood stove. She was distraught. Claude was like a son to her. Flames were pouring out and the clothes Stevens had dropped in a heap on the floor were now gone. He walked through the brittle midnight across to the bar. George Nielsen mixed him a drink. Liz came over from the house with the dread in her now too, and told Stevens, "You'd better get out of here, we don't know what frame of mind the boy is in."

At one o'clock Stevens pulled up in front of his trailer home on the potato farm, but the night was still not finished with him. He found a green box of .38 shells in the truck, six of which Dallas had used to kill the game wardens. It was evidence, and he had an alibi and a family to protect, so he buried the box out by a telephone pole. Inside his wife, Sandra, had awakened, wondering why he was back so soon. He told her the alibi. She looked into his eyes and said, "You're lying." "Go to bed," he said. He took another shower and joined her. But he couldn't sleep.

At first light he was outside, not quite sure how to clean the Blazer. It was simple, but until he recruited his son Darren's help, the task was too overwhelming. Too haunted. On the front seat lay the .357 revolver that Nielsen had given him for signals and which Dallas had handled on the ride out. It was a stark reminder that his alibi had fractures. His wife had instantly detected the flaws. The law would, too, when they came. He dug up the box of shells and shortly after dawn drove to Paradise Hill to return the evidence. The Nielsens were up and invited the farmer in for a mug of coffee. "Are you going to stick with the story?" George Nielsen tested him.

"Yeah," said Stevens. "I guess I've got to." But he was filled with pause. People said of Nielsen that he didn't know the difference between a lie and the sunshine, he was an alcoholic and "the king of bullshit." It would be easy for him, but for Stevens the lie was an ocean. He would drown in it. Without drinking his coffee, the farmer departed.

As he pulled onto his road, Stevens's children were being picked up by the schoolbus. Life seemed normal. But it was badly skewed. There was still blood in the rear of the Blazer. What was wrong? Sandra asked. What the hell was wrong? He ran water into a dishpan with soap to clean the Blazer and seal the lie. But in the end he couldn't maintain the silence and fiction. It was just a few hours later that he walked into the Humboldt County sheriff's office in Winnemucca, along with the Nielsens and an attorney.

Two hundred empty miles northeast of Winnemucca and a time zone away, sat the town of Murphy, Idaho, population fifty. Its one museum, one restaurant, one gas station, one public telephone, and one parking meter with a single clean bullet hole through the fifty-minute mark owed their existence to the one-story courthouse building that served as the seat of law and order for Owyhee County. From this desolate scatter of amenities, Sheriff Tim Nettleton enforced law in a territory larger than its namesake, Hawaii. Tall and rangy, Nettleton looked and strode and slung slow western adages the way a desert lawman ought to. In front of the courthouse a five-hundred-dollar reward poster for cattle rustlers displayed ranchers' brands like so many hieroglyphics. A glass showcase at the entrance to Nettleton's office was filled with confiscated drug paraphernalia and marked with the legend "Help Hang a Hippie Week." He had the necessary credentials; he was a local, independent and rustic. And yet he was savvy to the times. The Cessna 175 he flew to patrol his mammoth county was often parked right across from the courthouse. And his yard-long bookshelf was packed with volumes of Idaho law he had learned to read while studying business in college.

It was not yet three in the afternoon when Nettleton received a phone call from Frank Weston, a decent, harried-looking man who was sheriff at the far end of the Owyhee Desert, in Winnemucca. A potato farmer and a bar owner and his wife had showed up in Weston's office claiming that two game wardens had been shot down in one of Nettleton's canyons. It was a wild tale and unspecific. The region in question was terra incognita, conceptually no different from the menacing White Spaces left blank on frontier maps. Not only was it a vast and remote desert uninhabited during the winter except by game animals, coyotes, and wild horses, and during the summer by a handful of cowboys and cattle, the area at issue also fell within an ambiguous circle in which Idaho, Oregon, and Nevada join, the ION region. Though Stevens and Nielsen were vague about the location of Bull Camp and couldn't specify which fork of the convoluted Owyhee River it lay on, jurisdiction seemed to belong to Nettleton. Landmarks were rare: a cabin at the bottom of a ten-foot hole known as Devil's Corral, a windmill on the far ridge. Even Dallas, the pathfinder, had gotten lost on their initial caravan run back in early December. While Nettleton knew the county well ("I've lived long enough on that mountain . . . I haven't walked every inch of this ground, but I've ridden within fifty foot of it"), Bull Camp remained indistinct. After two hours of wrangling details and with night dropping fast, the sheriff took off in his Cessna in search of the alleged murder site. Working off gut instinct, he tried the South Fork first, and almost immediately found Bull Camp on the canyon floor. From the air he could see a white canvas tent near the thin river, and high above on the rim a pickup truck. By now it was far too dark to attempt a landing on the sagebrush plateau, and so he flew back to Murphy.

The brush was still glazed with frost when Nettleton returned next morning with a team of deputies and investigators and descended on foot into the deep canyon. The campsite was empty. The mules were running loose, the pelts were gone, and the trapline waited, jaws wide. There was not a soul to be found. In the tent, grain lay spilled on the ground, proof of Stevens's excitement. Shells for a .22 scattered on the mattress spoke of Dallas's cool frenzy as he readied his trap rifle for the finishing shots. Quickly Nettleton read the camp's character, accumulating a portrait. The sheriff had visited many camps and recognized them as signatures. This was a poacher's camp, you could tell by the way the man had baited his trapsets with exposed venison. Trash trapping, it's called, which translates as artless and rapacious. Nevertheless, the camp itself was manicured and clean, a mark of pride and discipline and care. The sheriff noticed that. He admired a well-kept camp and always took pleasure in visiting Basques on the range: a clean people who lived clean. Trappers were a different matter. When the season was on, some were neat . . . and this Dallas was the neatest he had seen . . . and some cared for nothing but the killing and skinning. Ironically this was the only trapper's camp Nettleton had ever visited in which the smell of death was absent.

By now it was known which two game wardens were missing (and Nettleton had long counted Bill Pogue as a personal friend). But with no bodies to show, the actual fate of the two men remained a matter of testimony. On foot the lawmen hunted for evidence. Beneath the scorch marks where Dallas had set fires, blood that had soaked into the earth was later typed to match Bill Pogue's and Conley Elms's. Still later, they attempted to locate slugs by using the metal detector Jim Stevens had brought for pioneer relics. There had been gunplay and blood, that much was established. But it remained only the word of a potato farmer and a bar owner with an appetite for lying that some character named Claude Dallas had done the killing or even that the wardens were dead. Fanning out, they found more traps, and in them several animals: a dead raccoon, a live bobcat, a golden eagle. None of the traps was marked with an identification number or the trapper's name. More men arrived to search for the game wardens, among them Michael Elms, Conley's stocky, bearded older brother. Michael Elms was the warden in charge of this district. Had he not been ill two days earlier, it would have been he at Bull Camp instead of his brother. They had grown up together on a small ranch in Beaver Marsh, Oregon, population twenty, working with their father at felling and sawing into lumber the lodgepole pines that grew on their property. Conley had been a gentle man. He and his wife were in the final stages of adopting a baby from India.

That afternoon a television helicopter from Boise spotted an enormous, nude body floating a quarter-mile downriver from the campsite, and Michael Elms's search came to an abrupt halt. It was too late to evacuate the body from Bull Camp, and so a guard was posted and vigil kept. Conley Elms was given one final night in the Owyhee wilderness.

On Thursday, four days after the murders, the sheriff from Owyhee County arrived in Winnemucca to compare notes and contribute whatever else he could to the ballooning manhunt. What Nettleton found was "a Chinese fire drill," a huge beast with too many heads craning after too many scents. "We had people walking on people," acknowledged Stan Rorex, Humboldt County's rawboned sheriff's investigator. By coincidence, three investigators for Nevada Narcotics and Investigation had been in town working on a sledgehammer-murder case, when the news broke of a cop killing at Bull Camp. Immediately they had offered their services. Next day the FBI had called with an offer of assistance, SWAT teams and a helicopter. Fish and Game officers from Idaho had appeared from nowhere to help, and also to hector for more and faster results. Even the air force chipped in. In the space of thirty hours nearly a dozen local, state, and federal agencies had jumped on the wagon. There were thirty lawmen by the second of January; fifty by the third. For a department attuned to a slower, bucolic rhythm, the sudden massing of lawmen was nerve-wracking. The science of good police work was being applied, questions answered, data compiled (especially after the FBI arrived), but Claude Dallas was still out there and they had not managed to find the body of Bill Pogue.

Nettleton's first instinct was to get a tracker. "I should have ignored all the safety rules," Nettleton said. "I should have brought down a deputy named Jack out of Canyon County [Idaho] who can track anything. At the time Jack wanted to follow the prints on out and see if we couldn't pick the sign up west of there." Several lawmen had already studied the spot on Sand Pass Road where Dallas had supposedly been let off, and found human footprints leading north into the Bloody Run Hills. But the prints could just as well have belonged to chukar hunters as Dallas. It was a snowless January and that served to hinder the hunt. Not only was there no snow in which to read prints, but the ground had been frozen tight the night Dallas vanished, a poor bed for tracks. On top of that it was shirt-sleeves weather during the day, one further advantage for a fugitive on foot. Dogs were brought in, but they failed to catch a definitive scent. By the time Nettleton showed up, the trail that may have belonged to Dallas was soupy with extraneous prints, and the single thread that might have led to the fugitive was abandoned. Winter sunsets and rumor sealed shut behind him like a maze. Thereafter, the search reduced to a quiltwork of probes and deduction.

In the beginning, the slayer was virtually a cipher. In the earliest news account of the murders, buried deep in the story, the suspect appeared only as a thirty-year-old trapper, a deft gunsmith and knifemaker of mysterious proportions. The image titillated, even if it lacked dimension. There wasn't enough yet to visualize what Dallas looked like, what sort of hat he wore, whether he was like the man who had recently shotgun-ned a family in neighboring Pershing County, or a mad hermit like the neanderthal "Bristlewolf," who had burrowed into a dugout in the Black Rock Desert and subsisted on the raw flesh of highway kills until the day he shot two hikers and a pros-pector. Possibly he was something more or different. The name itself was a cue, though. Claude Dallas. It was secular and blunt, with dirt beneath its nails. That he was young and wielded bygone skills were promising seeds, too; and on the fourth morning after the murders, the *Idaho Statesman* spawned a portrait so rich with color it almost defied ordinary newsprint.

"Claude knows every damn gopher hole and cave in the Northwest," opened a quote. A first-rate outdoorsman, a crack shot, a white-water canoeist, a survival expert, Dallas was "per-fectly at home in the bitter winter cold of the desert." He was better than good copy, he was a renaissance man of the West. His basics were given, five feet ten and 170 pounds, and his brown shoulder-length hair was tied back in a ponytail. He had a beard and brown eyes. Change the color of his eyes and hair and he was Jeremiah Johnson, a fictional broth of real mountain men. "A tough little turkey," Sheriff Weston summarized for reporters. "He knows the area like his own living room. He loves guns and has plenty of ammunition. I imagine we'll have to take him the hard way." Other law officials anticipated the trapper's appeal and curtly dismissed him as a "creep" and a "renegade." They weren't just searching for Dallas, they were "hungry" for him. He had enemies, they were singing, many and well armed. And he was just a lone man, "not a big man," as a local recollected in some frontier bar in whiskey-and-horses McDermitt, Nevada. "But he's healthy and hearty. I'll bet he could go sixty miles on foot in one night." Twenty miles, amended Nettleton. Two hundred, expanded another voice. "If they want to catch him," said the cowboy, "they'll have to check the Canadian border. He might be there by now." Intoned the article, "Other bar patrons listened as he talked. And when he said he hoped Dallas would escape, [they] nodded agreement." He may not have been a big man, but suddenly Dallas was larger than life. Sixty miles in a night. Two hundred! The man wore seven-league boots. Each morning thereafter, the mountain man was nourished with further embellishments. A survival expert was interviewed, and he presented the desertscape as a veritable grocery store stocked with sego lily bulbs and biscuit-root plants and fresh high protein, tasty meats caught nightly in snares. Water was no problem, even where the streambeds were dry. Frost could be wiped off plant leaves with a handkerchief and squeezed into a container; ice could be chipped off rocks and melted over a fire. While the reader drank his breakfast coffee, it was easy to picture Claude smacking his lips over the feast he was treading upon.

"He was the only guy we ever had who wore a gun all the time, even just driving a tractor or truck," said a farmhand north of Winnemucca. "It was a .357 Magnum and, oh, I wouldn't want him shooting at me. He could hit that pole [about seventy yards away] nine times out of ten." The estimate was bettered. "That son of a bitch could shoot the eye out of a needle at two hundred fifty yards," swore a friend. It was said that the sole eyewitness to the Bull Camp doings, Jim Stevens, had taken to wearing a bulletproof jacket everywhere.

While the manhunt flooded across the terrain "hungry" for the capture, Dallas was sighted elsewhere, on the pages of a National Geographic Society book entitled *The American Cowboy,* published in 1972. People looked and there was Claude, younger and beardless and hunkered down in his leather chaps with a sprawled crew of buckaroos in one photo, and in another riding full page toward the viewer, one of five men abreast in their ankle-length slickers. Except for the peach fuzz and wire rims, he was the Marlboro man. The FBI was reportedly trying to learn how Dallas had spent the first twenty years of his life. According to neighbors, the boy had appeared ten years ago, riding a horse and leading a pair of pack mules. But he'd never really said where he was from, which served to deepen his quaint mystery. And when finally the *Statesman* located his parents in South Carolina, their contribution was summarily rustic. "We're all tore up," said his father. "But we're standing close by him." In spare, backwoods code, it confirmed what others had already said, that the boy was "quiet, shy, dependable, and a good-hearted man." He was worth standing by. People said so.

"I hunt a lot," said Jim Calder, Dallas's dentist and an acquaintance of Bill Pogue's. "I've come across Claude out in the desert lots of times. He has camps all over this country. As well as I know him, I always got the cold shoulder when I met him in the desert. Probably why he didn't like you coming around was he always had a deer or something he'd shot out of season in his camp. There's no secret about that. He either didn't want you to see what he had shot, or he didn't want you to be implicated if he got in trouble for it. I don't know which. I do know Claude believed he had a right to kill animals out of season without regard for game laws." Of itself, his poaching was no felony: game laws were simple misdemeanors. And besides, he had a communion with the desert, knew his guns, and could ride. "Claude's lived the kind of life most of us only wish we could live," summarized Cortland Nielsen, crusty George's brother and a friend to Dallas. "He knows the cowboy life. He knows about open country and taking care of himself." Alone, the young mountain man faced all odds now. And though they might despise what he had done . . . capping two men in the dirt . . . still the ION people were drawn to the solitary figure. The attraction was natural, culturally irresistible. Solitude, independence, the ability to go it alone. For most of a century the cowboy and his flamekeepers had been mourning the lost, titanic days. Here was a titan though, part buckaroo, part gunslinger, part mountain man and free trapper, quiet, shy, dependable, and a good-hearted man.

The lawmen were prepared to fight the fugitive with police science and high-powered weaponry and the law, but they weren't ready to fight his epiphany. They didn't mean to . . . they explicitly meant not to . . . but the lawmen fed the romanticism, too. Their language and dress and discoveries all elucidated the rough frontier romance. Dallas was called a rattlesnake ("Leave me strictly alone," Nettleton characterized him, "and I'll leave you alone"), a dog, a horse thief. Lawmen had whiskey bet on his capture. When Stan Rorex, the sheriff's investigator, rappeled down into rotting mine shafts and caves, he found snakes, rusty ore cars, and old dynamite. A news photo showed Rorex stepping wide past a wind-shattered cabin, his bootcut jeans taut on the thigh and work-shirt sleeves rolled up, packing a gun on his hip and a heavy rifle in his square hands. And never absent in the background was the Country.

They did what they could to cripple the incipient myth. The director of Idaho's Fish and Game Department, Jerry Conley, went to great lengths to degrade a rumor that Claude had been acting in self-defense. "It was not spur of the moment or a fit of passion," he insisted. "It is my opinion that a mailman collecting four cents would have been killed." Toward further hamstringing the image of a desperate and freedom-loving loner, he revealed that Dallas had "told other people in the area he thought it would be a lot of fun to be pursued by officers, going from cache of weapons to cache of weapons . . . and fighting it out." A well-established potato farmer on the far side of Sand Pass Road, Jerry Brinkerhoff, gave further voice to an eccentric rather than muscular Dallas. "Claude showed me a gas mask one time. Claude sometimes talked about the next war. He said you had to have that kind of stuff for the future. He said people with the right equipment would be able to go in the mountains and protect themselves."

There was no doubt that Dallas had possessed the right equipment. On the day before Conley Elms's body was spotted in the river, while the Nielsens and Jim Stevens were still being interviewed at the sheriff's office, Stan Rorex and several others had raided Paradise Hill. Heavily armed, they had searched an old, half-converted schoolbus, a car, and a trailer which the trapper had kept parked behind the bar. This first glimpse into the possessions and mind of the alleged murderer had confirmed his interest in mayhem. Stowed neatly and in immaculate condition were seven rifles, including an M16, ten handguns, a bulletproof vest, a gas mask, an Israeli tanker's helmet, cartridge reloaders, speed loaders for his handguns, knives, gun clips, and a small library on firearms, homemade machine guns and silencers, police and military technique, combat shooting, and quick draw. A new sealed case of between two thousand and three thousand .30 caliber bullets turned up, an ominous find, for none of the guns seized used that size load. There were rumors that Dallas had arms caches scattered throughout the desert, and the quantity of weaponry and ammunition lent a mystical credibility to this and darker tales.

Every visitor to the rural West has seen the open display of rifles in window racks and the bumper stickers that enunciate the credo "When the Man Comes for Your Gun, Give Him Both Barrels." But if the grimness with which men hold their weapons and legends of their weapons sacred is a cliché, it's anything but stale. What urbanites call arsenals are known more simply in Nevada and the ION region as gun collections. Even many of the lawmen saw nothing exceptional in the number of weapons found in Dallas's trailer and schoolbus. Almost anywhere else, the symbolic overkill of seventeen guns, thousands of rounds of ammunition, and a library devoted to deadly force, coupled with an eyewitness account of double homicide, would have met with shock and revulsion. Instead, here, the symbols validated him. Ever so lightly at first, a remarkable line was forming in ION minds. During the first days, few could see the fault line, but it cracked deeper and deeper.

Steve Bishop, the county's huge undersheriff, saw it in the first hour or so, though he had no way of knowing how profound it would become. He had been present as Jim Stevens, still white with fear, and the raspy-voiced bar owner and his wife committed to tape their versions of the terrible night.

They were all going to jail, or so Stevens and Liz Nielsen and all the lawmen thought. To Bishop's amazement, however, well before the initial interviews were even complete, the district attorney was indicating that the Nielsens and Stevens were not to be arrested. Bishop was shocked, for at the time Humboldt County was holding prisoner an eyewitness to the sledgehammer murder, an impoverished wetback who couldn't speak English, had no relatives or friends in the country, and couldn't possibly raise bond. The man would spend over four hundred days in jail waiting for trial. There were understandable fears that this key witness might flee the country once released, but the point was, he was innocent. George Nielsen, on the other hand, had thrown bloody boots and other evidence into a garbage can, and had driven Dallas to a drop-off point and then probably lied about where it was. His wife had stuffed evidence into her kitchen fire. And as for Stevens, there were no guarantees he hadn't pulled the trigger at Bull Camp himself. And yet they were walking free. The DA reportedly joked he couldn't arrest Liz Nielsen because the hospital needed its head nurse too badly. More formally, he reasoned, all three had acted under duress and coercion. Yet nearly eleven hours had lapsed before the sheriff's office was contacted, and even then George Nielsen had been late getting to town because he was "tied up with a deliveryman." The range and degrees of duress would normally have been up to a court to decipher. No court was involved. They walked free.

Whether the absence of arrest, much less prosecution, was a nod to the community's independence or contributed to it, the statement was clear. A different sort of law applied in cow counties. Law had always been a starving animal in northern Nevada. Where it existed at all, it had traditionally been underrepresented, underfunded, and largely unwelcome. "One thing we have out here," explained a sheriff, "is people taking care of their own problems. Somebody takes something, they'll go get it back. And take a pound of flesh, too." "Live and let live," commands the governor on the back of the state road map. Every lawman in the region shoulders that attitude as one more part of the geography, the same as the long distances between ranches. "What might take five minutes in the city can take two or three hours up here," said Rorex. "You might end up helping them round up their cattle before you get your information. You might walk in and they'll say I don't want to talk about it right now, come on in and let's eat or have some coffee. You talk about the weather or his wife having a baby or a neighbor's cows and three hours later you get the information you came for. You don't pressure them. You just have to be sort of easygoing, the see-you-mañana type." It would dog the investigators, frustrate and outrage the more law-abiding community in Boise, and ultimately help the tales of Claude Dallas breed with the larger mythos of the old West. What first erupted upon the terrain and the people as a cold-blooded slaughter quickly retracted into ritual and defensiveness. By no means did everyone defend Dallas, but the mood was protective. The community was defending itself, for Dallas had stood for much of what they stood for.

He was a buckaroo, a trapper, a truck driver, a well driller. That signified their own simple union with the land, their collaboration with the isolation. Informed by his instincts and the pool of knowledge that has helped so many in the ION region survive, Dallas had done well enough in country that once struck California-bound immigrants as a sustained disaster. By coastal America's standards, the cow counties are out of synch, even anticontemporary. "Hell," marveled one deputy. "There are still people in some of the back country who don't even

know Disneyland exists." Old-fashioned and physical, the people understand that the land is preeminent and that without it
they would be sailors without a sea. Their connection with the
earth and its creatures keeps them almost tribal. Dallas addressed them with an elder voice, in the poetics of outlawry.
From Paradise Valley to Burns, Oregon, and back south again
to Eureka, Nevada, you could practically hear the ghosts of
mountain men, miners, and cowboys slapping off the dust.

For all the lawmen knew that first week, Hugh Glass or Joe
Meek or Jim Bridger, with a neck thicker around than his skull,
or any other of the giant mountain men really *was* striding
through the desert outback and beyond, haunting the atrophied
wilderness. He could have been anywhere. A Nevada game
warden named Gene Weller who had dealt with the cagey
trapper before estimated that Dallas's range extended from Eureka to Idaho. The more they learned, the farther the range
extended. He had buckarooed in Oregon, canoed in the Northwest Territories and the Yukon, hitchhiked through every state
of the Union. But in the beginning, because there was nowhere
else so tangible, they concentrated on the area four prospectors
had long ago labeled Paradise.

It is a twenty-mile-wide floor bracketed by bunches of
mountains that jut up and just as abruptly plummet back into
the piedmont. These small clusters of mountains box Paradise
in like edges of the world. Time stops here, checked at the
cattle guards as you enter the little town of Paradise Valley
(shrunken from the grandiose Paradise City of the late nine-
teenth century). One cattle guard vibrates your tires. The other
is just white stripes on the asphalt, enough to worry most cows.
Old cowhide, prescribed to shy horses away, rots on the grating
that borders the guards, and you can't help but slow down from
75 mph to 1930 or 1890, or earlier still. Paradise Valley is at

once an outpost in time and a capital for the ranches, both family-operated and corporate-owned, tucked invisibly here and there on the valley floor. The raffle prize at the annual Volunteer Firemen's Dance is still the front and rear quarters of a cow. Survival is for the fittest, the most savvy, no different for today's market-embattled stockman than for yesterday's line rider; you outthink and outlast the bad weather and the harsh land, or you're just not around at the end of the winter. The most commonly reckoned consolation is that economic recovery is just around the corner. These are stayers and this is 20 Mule Team, Reagan country. In Paradise Valley one person was on unemployment insurance, no more. That's statistics, northern Nevada style. They take care of their own. "If there's a fist fight in a place like the bar in Paradise Valley," remarked Rorex, "they don't even bother to call the sheriff. They either take care of it themselves or somebody goes home with a broken arm." They had a deputy posted in Paradise a few years back, but he lasted less than a month before the community had him recalled.

Into this anachronism descended the forces of law in search of Claude Dallas and his victim, Bill Pogue. The ranchers and buckaroos watched as the tracking dogs came up empty along the Bloody Run Hills, and a sonar probe beneath the ice at Chimney Creek Dam failed to produce silhouettes even faintly resembling a man's body. The manhunt had top priority, but the search for Pogue was important, too. Eddie Pogue, the warden's younger brother, had showed up, a forceful reminder that the family in Boise was in agony over the absence of Bill Pogue's remains. Missing also was an answer to the riddle of why Dallas had transported the corpse *out* of the wilderness, especially after having to leave one body in the river and the destruction of evidence incomplete. From the amount of gas

missing from George Nielsen's normally full truck, it was calculated that Dallas could have dropped the body off anywhere
within a forty-mile radius. It was probable that Dallas had
stayed on some road, though with the earth frozen hard, he
could as easily have driven the body almost anywhere within
sixteen hundred square miles.

Returning to Chimney Creek Dam with his scuba gear,
Rorex dove through a suspicious hole in the eight-inch-thick
ice. The water was that brackish, alkaline Humboldt water so
despised and yet welcomed by pioneers, and he could barely
see his light even when pressed against his face mask. Wearing
a harness and rope, he descended and felt cautiously among the
rocks for a body. A cowboy line shack, fences, and a corral had
all been covered over by the reservoir, and he had no idea what
might lie at the bottom. For an hour he stayed down, searching
for soft flesh. Then, in total darkness, he felt his leg hugged
tight and had to wrestle free of rotting willows on the floor. He
had had enough of the bottom and emerged into the chill air.
Ultrasonic devices were lowered through auger holes drilled in
the ice, to no effect. Next day a diver searched the spillway
below Bilk Creek Reservoir. At the suggestion of the first of
many psychics, a gravel pit on Highway 95 was partially exca-
vated with a front-end loader. Caves and mine shafts were
searched. A natural hot springs by the Four R Ranch was
pumped low by the National Guard on the theory that Dallas
might have boiled the bones clean in its mineral waters. As
night came on, a boat was lowered into the steaming, caver-
nous pit, and with the aid of a searchlight a guardsman probed
with a pole while he floated with the underground currents.
The steam scalded him so badly that he couldn't shave for a
week, and all he got for his troubles were beer kegs, wire, old
traps, and a cow skull. Ghost towns and line shacks and
wasted, forgotten cabins were searched. Nothing.

In the state of Nevada, Dallas was guilty of no more than a few misdemeanors: transportation of a body without a license, burying a body without embalming it, and burial at an improper location. By crossing the state line, however, he had committed interstate flight, and that opened the door wide to the FBI. On January 8, two five-man SWAT teams, one from Las Vegas and one from Reno, began a businesslike sweep of the areas in which Dallas was known to have traveled and trapped. Using a Huey helicopter, they eliminated spot after spot from their map of suspicions, landing at mine shafts and caves. Other FBI agents began to interview some of the people of Paradise Valley, searching for clues. Already they had background notes on Dallas, for as it turned out they had arrested him in 1973 for draft evasion. On that occasion FBI Agent Eric Neale had disguised himself as a ranch hand and, with two other lawmen, had taken Dallas as he was sacking a colt, breaking it to the saddle. In short, the FBI had mug shots and fingerprints of Dallas in their files, a useful acquaintance.

As the SWAT teams worked the hot spots and agents harvested information from Paradise Valley and Paradise Hill and elsewhere, the sheriff's office joined the manhunt, armed with a variety of high-powered automatic and semiautomatic weapons, bulletproof vests and helmets. This was resoundingly Dallas's high ground. He held the advantages. "We figured he might get one or two of us," said Rorex. "And we wanted weapons that could really reach out there and shoot back with." When they came to mining mills with menacing complexes of buildings, they patched together military tactics and took each structure by storm. "There were several eerie times," said Rorex, "when we felt we weren't alone out there." There was fear. Dallas was a legend. He could live like an animal. And he hated the law. At one point a young Paradise trapper named Ken Klaumann spied human tracks at the base of a remote

overhang and reported them. Later that week, Klaumann followed the tire tracks of a deputy's truck out toward the site and
was surprised to see them stop short of the overhang, well out
of rifle range, and turn around.

At dawn on Thursday morning, January 8, an Idaho Forest
Service airplane flew along the Bloody Run range behind Paradise Hill and took a series of infrared photos in search of heat
pools. Figuring Dallas was too smart to build a fire at night,
they thought he might try to warm himself at sunrise, when
neither the fire's glow nor the smoke would show. The photos
showed several illuminated spots. Each was checked. One was
a Southwest Gas pumping station. None was Dallas. Because
the expense seemed unjustified and it was increasingly likely
the fugitive was gone from the territory, the plane and its camera returned to Idaho. The manhunt would continue for several
more days, but after Thursday its size quickly dwindled. The
SWAT teams returned to their bases, Fish and Game officers
went home. Nettleton flew back to Murphy.

That night, fifty miles west of Paradise near the Black Rock
Desert, in the middle of a ten-day circle on foot, Claude Dallas
got cold. He built a fire by a scooped-out depression in the soil,
warmed himself, and cooked some meat. In the morning he
pulled branches over the hollow and slept. He was surrounded
by illusions. The mountain ridges were so white they blended
with the clouds, and what started as roots of dark, heavy stone
magically took flight. The water he drank sprang from nowhere
and went nowhere; on waterway maps which show the great
rivers of the continent as long, intricate branches of lightning,
the Humboldt River is a twig that issues from places like Paradise Valley, then forks southward into utter blankness, disap-
pearing into the Carson Sink. Sometimes the illusions yield

secrets, sometimes they make a fool of you or kill you. Build a logical, straight fence between two points and, unless you can see the illusion, you may have just stranded your cattle on the far side of a snowdrift come winter, where they'll starve to death. It has happened. The illusions are older than logic. In 1913 a fire was spotted not far from Bull Camp in the Owyhee. It went on for day after day and made no sense, a steady plume of smoke where there were no trees to burn and no people to tend a fire. Finally several curious buckaroos investigated and were astonished to find a volcano, or its remains, for it had already extinguished itself and receded into illusion. They marveled at the hot lava.

On Thursday night the orange wink of a fire was reported out by Geneva Springs. It made no sense, though. There were far more logical places to check. Two months passed before a BLM crew happened across the cold ashes by a hollow in the earth. By then, of course, Dallas was gone.

# Chapter 3

**H**IS spoor traced back through the years . . . shadows and mirror images, echoes and posturings. The high desert asceticism, the rawhide-and-bullets solitude, even the dislike for game laws were all moments repeated like a litany from his boyhood in Ohio. The books he read as a youngster were prints that fit his adult foot exactly, patterns leading forward to Bull Camp and backward to grander, more heroic times.

"Our part of the valley," read one tract, "was as American as America could be. It was as Middle West as Middle West could get. It was beautiful, I think, in a quiet way." Becalmed in just such a pastoral latitude, the schoolboy Claude studied those whisperings from Edison Marshall's *The Heart of the Hunter*, a wilderness autobiography. "At that early age I had not yet isolated the fact, although I had seen its signs, that hunting is a lonely sport, that the hunter is essentially a lonely man . . . and the bigger the game, the lonelier it gets." Like a monk of the jungle or tundra or desert, the hunter exposed himself to extraordinary, basic truths, and they all reduced to Darwin's ditty: The fittest survive. "It was the way of life, and it was just," another favorite, Jack London, instructed the boy in tenth grade. "[The hunter] had been born close to the earth, close to the earth had he lived, and the law thereof was not new to him. It was the law of all flesh. And nature was not kindly to the flesh." Men who understood that primal lesson stood simple and wise, resigned to cycling through the hardships endlessly.

Dallas entered the cycle on March 11, 1950, in Winchester, Virginia, and was named for his father, a hardworking jack-of-all-trades. The family was large and Catholic, migrating from Ohio where the father had a job with Firestone as a chemical engineer to a dairy farm in the upper peninsula of northern Michigan, then to Mount Gilead in central Ohio in 1962, where Claude Senior worked for the state on bridge design and construction. With the move to Mount Gilead, the younger Claude, never a large or conspicuous boy, fell prey to a double anonymity; he became an unknown face in a small, close-knit town, and furthermore an unknown face among hundreds of other unknown faces flooding Morrow County, sons and daughters of a startling oil strike. Stilled for generations by their peace with the soil, farmers, dairymen, and townspeople alike were electrified when oil was suddenly discovered beneath their croplands. The fever hit fast. Where three or four lots touched, there were three or four wells, each neighbor furiously pulling at the single oil pool beneath their adjoining land until the pool went dry. County roads were drenched with salt water sucked from the ground, ostensibly to keep the dust down but in fact just to dump the by-product. Finally the salt water leached out into the fields and fouled the ditch water and the plant life and crops started dying. There were rigs everywhere. A well was even drilled on home plate of the school baseball diamond. Roughnecks from Illlinois and West Virginia and the deeper South, as faraway as Texas, appeared, and their gypsy children glutted the schools. They had short roots, fast lives. Attendance books were filled with rows of names of schoolchildren who started in September, then simply vanished. There was nothing unique or colorful about young Claude, he was part and parcel of the bustling, exotic horde.

A reticent family guided by Appalachian pride and conviction, the Dallases looked no farther than the walls of their frame house for security. With the muscles of his back and two hands and his secular knowledge of the land, physics, and animals, Claude Dallas, Sr., provided for the six boys and three girls and their mother, a small, feisty dynamo of a woman. He taught the virtues of hard work. "I don't know if I'm going to have any earthly possessions to leave my kids when I'm dead and gone," he said, "but figured if I left the world of work and the knowledge that they should be honest, then I'd done the best I could for them. That's worth more than money." He exposed his sons to trapping, guns, and hunting, crafts that represented the frontier to his second oldest son and namesake. "From the time that boy was old enough to want to do," said his father, "five, six years old, he talked about the West. I don't know why, but he sure had a hankering for it." Claude shot his first deer at age nine. "He shot a thirty-odd-six," his father remembered. "I was proud of him, and he was awfully proud of hisself." While other students played football or worked on the yearbook or talked cars and women, Dallas soberly ran his traplines, taking fox, raccoon, muskrat, and, rarely, a mink. "He was just a woodsman from the day go," said a classmate, David Hartpence. He was shy, "the most silent guy in the class," and he dressed like a character out of Hemingway. Any day of the year he could be depended on to be wearing a flannel shirt, and if it wasn't freshly washed blue jeans with work boots, then it was work boots with dress pants. His hair was closely cropped in a crew cut. He was a clean, pragmatic, earnest-looking boy who kept his mouth closed even when he smiled. He didn't date. Bright but unacademic (he ranked sixty-fifth out of eighty in his graduating class), he never seemed to consider going to college. Even so, he promised his mother he would finish high school. And then, emphatically, "as soon as he graduated he was going to the Rocky Mountains," said Hartpence. "He had that dream from the start. He wanted to get established as a mountain man."

The closest you get to the Wild West in central Ohio are the mock gunfights at the Olentangy Indian Caverns north of Columbus and Pony Express motifs on the mud flaps of eighteen-wheelers delivering produce. All the same, uniformed in his flannel shirts and backwoods smile, the adolescent fur trapper hunted and cached frontier rhythms. "Strictly outdoors," his father observed. "He lived on the creek and the river." The first time Claude heard a song called "North to Alaska," he turned to his father and said, "Dad, that's where I'm going." Much of the fantasy was made from books. "He read a lot," said his father. "He read constantly. Zane Grey and Jack London and novels like such." Sometimes he checked the same library book out twice, the better to engrain its imagery. His literary interests were undeviating: the West, the wilderness, adventure. Besides London and Grey, he read *Toward Oregon* (by E.

H. Staffelbach), *The Horsemen of the Plains* (Joseph Altsheler), *The White Feather* (Merritt Allen), and Andy Adams's classic *The Log of a Cowboy.* A poetry began to build. With picture documentaries, he took imaginary excursions to Alaska, boned up on African, Indian, and Burmese big-game hunting, and studied the West with Louis L'Amour and with Owen Wister's *The Virginian.* With *The Heart of the Hunter,* something bordering on destiny mounted the boy's fantasies.

In it, Claude met Charles Cottar, a real African guide of the twenties and thirties described as "hickory tough . . . probably the greatest hunter on earth." Though he had "piercing eyes, narrow set, indescribably blue," narrated the author, "still I did not know that he was the heir of Jim Bridger and Kit Carson, the very last of that great breed of hunters developed in the American West. A true Mountain Man born after his proper time . . ." Following an unannounced change in the game rules, an African game warden confiscated from this true mountain man a rhino head. Worse yet, the warden pompously dressed Cottar down, prompting the author to wonder, "what would have happened if [the warden] had said [these things] away from his desk out on the veld, when Cottar was not belittled and bewildered . . . by the fences of civilization he could not cope with or understand." Out there, in places remote, on the veld or tundra or desert where nothing insulated men from nature's unkindly laws, "I think Cottar would have thrown [the warden] down and given him the kiboko [a heavy whip made of hippo hide]." It was just a small remark buried in a large book, and there is no way of knowing if Dallas made the connection between this game warden and the two he killed at Bull Camp.

Class by class, the Vietnam War had begun to devour the boys of Mount Gilead High School. The casualties were numerous and tangible; Ohio had one of the highest rates of war dead in the country. In 1967 the norm was not protest or resistance. If you were male and eighteen, you went to college or you went into the military. When a local boy dared to quit the Air Force Academy and fled to Canada, Mount Gilead was scandalized. There was a sense, not of desperation, but of immediacy as high-school seniors scrambled for entrance to colleges or simply surrendered themselves to the current and were drafted. "I can't remember Claude ever talking about Vietnam, though," said Hartpence, whose own brother was killed there. "Claude was going to the Rockies, that was it."

At one time boys scarcely older than Dallas had been so hungry for information about the poorly charted, savage . . . and exploitable . . . interior that, as fast as they appeared in libraries, fresh government publications on Frémont's westward passage were stolen for reference. Soaked in fictions of the fabulous West, young Claude looked around him at the landscape of Ohio, a humid land of rivers and trees, where the townships press up on one another like fallen dominoes and the land is on its knees, a servant to the farmers, and the cattle are so tame and familiar that they never feel the heat of a brand. *It was as Middle West as Middle West could get.* Above the John Deere threshers and red-and-white barns, the sky had no character, the sunsets were chinless, and the horizon mussy with foliage. From just such a purgatory, teenage boys had fled a century and more earlier. Of all his male classmates bound for college or the Asian jungle, Claude alone wore an old-fashioned bow tie for his senior photograph. And above the bow tie, the boy's eyes were alive. In the spring of that year, Dallas fulfilled his promise to graduate, and soon after vaulted into the hinterland, almost, but not quite, never to be heard of again. "He didn't leave with any prejudice, you know," said his father.

"I was willing. In fact, I was glad to see him make the trip. He wanted it so awful bad."

On a circuitous route, first driving an old, painted truck through the South and then hitchhiking on toward the Pacific coast, Dallas spent the summer edging westward. He was ripe for an odyssey and basked in small, parochial adventures. "Cops tried to run him in for vagrancy," a cowboy friend later recalled. "He got picked up by all kinds of weirdos, he slept under park benches. But he stuck 'er out. He had his mind made up he was coming out west." A half-sister lived in California, which made it convenient for him, in his own colloquial reckoning, "to winter out of San Jose" that year, feeding cattle on a dairy farm. As the Tet offensive ground down overseas, spring appeared, and around the time of his eighteenth birthday, Dallas resumed the voyage, searching for a summit.

Carrying an old army pack forty pounds heavy (with which he could, he claimed, cover forty miles in a day "if I run a little"), he hitchhiked onward. One fateful night the tired traveler landed in a large orange orchard in Exeter, California, not far from Sequoia National Park. Next morning the owner, Jim Pogue (no relation to the game warden Bill Pogue), found the wayfarer in his grove and they struck up a conversation during which the boy's interest in ranching came out. By chance it turned out that Pogue had owned a ranch five years before. Surrounded by white orange blossoms, he tantalized the boy with its description. The most beautiful spot on earth, he promised, it's there at the Alvord Ranch in the sparsest outer limits of Oregon. Alvord: it was Pogue's word, Claude's image. That was enough. Dallas loaded up and headed off, into a region that was like the bottom of the ocean, its rotting volcanoes pressed flat and then suddenly springing high like Tetons with lush valleys that promptly fell again into harsh, white alkaline flats.

A buckaroo boss was driving his family to Burns, Oregon, in a pickup one June night, lashed by a rainstorm nobody had particularly wished for, when he spied a sturdy boy walking along the twenty-eight miles of dirt road from the highway, oblivious to the downpour. He was in search of the headquarters of the Alvord Ranch, he said, and the boss obligingly pointed downroad. Did he want a ride? No. He was just fine as is, and sank off into the storm. Next evening, for the first and possibly only time it was ever rung, the doorbell sounded at the Wilsons' ranchhouse on the Mann Lake Ranch, which included the Alvord Ranch. There stood a weathered but well-groomed young man shepherding a large khaki backpack and looking for work. Coco Wilson, a lively and genteel ranchwoman educated at the Chapin School in New York, invited the boy in, and when her son, Hoyt, returned, made the introductions. "We needed a man," said Hoyt Wilson, "so we put him to work. It was going to be just temporary. Just a week." He was set to tearing down old fence.

By thirteen, the sons of cowmen can repair tires, perform basic surgery on farm equipment, sharpen every tool imaginable, saddle a horse and ride it, and know by instinct which gate on the ranch's maze of fencework to keep closed and which to keep open. They can recite the number of head being run on their property, the number of riders and hands employed, give a history of the region and directions to anyplace within fifty miles, and know how to set posts and stretch wire and kill a rattlesnake with or without a gun. They have a bearing found in only the most street smart of gang members or among the children of diplomats posted overseas, a composure that comes from being thrown on your own devices. The muscle they lack is just a finishing touch, nothing good wits can't compensate for. Claude Dallas arrived in the ION region less capable than one of their children. He was barely eighteen, but many cowboys will tell you that eighteen is too old to learn. "There's some things that you have to be born with or be around when you're young," one buckaroo named Gary Rose explained. "It's tough for a guy. He comes in new and learns a little bit, then his pride gets in the way." The opportunity to cowboy was infinitely more important than pride, though, and Dallas hung on, tougher than he was green. Random as the Alvord Ranch was, it had not come into his life by accident. The Alvord was Mount Everest or a Rhodes scholarship or the Green Berets; it was the dream. He had been searching for the Alvord all his life.

Dallas toiled. In two days' time he had torn out all the old barbwire fence, so they sent him with a Basque boy and a failing Jeep pickup to a line cabin up "on the mountain," in this case literally a peak in the Steens Range, to repair sections of barbwire destroyed by the winter snows. "Resin jaw work," it's called, for the kind of broken-down, plug-tobacco-chewing old cowboy who normally performs it in lieu of retirement. At the end of the week the Basque boy descended alone, fed up. The truck had high-centered on a rock and the rear end was torn out, and as far as he was concerned that spelled a halt to the mission. Four days passed before Hoyt Wilson could get up to retrieve the truck. As the Dallas boy still had not showed up, he checked in at the cabin to rescue his missing worker. The boy was nowhere to be seen. It was eight in "the afternoon," then nine. At last, as the first stars lit up, Dallas appeared. Every morning before daylight he'd been packing seventy and eighty pounds of steel posts and barbwire on foot to a section five miles and a thousand vertical feet up the mountainside, then descending at dark. "We knew a good thing when we saw it," said Wilson. Dallas stayed for two years.

He was given an old packhorse and a saddle horse suitably gentle for a rookie who had never ridden. For the remainder of the summer and into the fall, the line cabin was his home. He had found the mythic pyramid, the very center of his continent, and he kept right on climbing. "First thing he did," recalled Wilson, "he sent away for a centennial thirty-thirty Winchester with a hexagonal barrel about thirty inches long. He packed that thing around with him when he was fixing fence, even though he couldn't hit the broad side of a barn because his eyes weren't very good. He'd pack that thing around and stand there with it in the crook of his arm."

He worked hard at the way it should be. Even before ordering the commemorative rifle, he found a rusty pistol in a bush on the mountain and labored to refurbish it. "He practiced," said Wilson. Despite his hobbled vision, "he got it down, sitting around on the porch of that cabin up there shooting at ground squirrels after hours in the evening." Before long he graduated to deer. As was standard for old-time buckaroos in the field, he ate a lot of venison through the summer and fall, poaching ignored. Outfitted with two horses and a gun, he was still short of his vision, still consigned to resin jaw work. Without a complaint, he paid his dues, setting fence until winter, then pitching hay through the snowy months. He was quiet and, in contrast to many of the hands, well mannered and drank very little. "I got to feeling like he was part of my family," said Coco Wilson, a remark that would resonate in other ION women's mouths.

In the spring of 1969 Dallas asked to become a buckaroo. "So we did it," said Hoyt Wilson. "We took him out riding." The grandeur and prestige of horsemanship are vestigial; in

Spanish *caballero,* or horseman, is synonymous with gentleman. *Peon* means pedestrian. While the convention has largely withered elsewhere in the face of machinery, there are still those in the ION region who argue that a true buckaroo never works on foot. "It's embarrassing getting off your horse and having him watch you do the work he's supposed to do," Gary Rose contended, loading his lip with chew. "Little things like that will ruin a horse."

The son of a rodeo hand, Rose and his bride, Becky, met Dallas when they were hired on to the six-man buckaroo crew at the Alvord Ranch for $250 a month. Living in a rock bunkhouse across from the cookhouse, the boy was as green as a spring twig. "But for a guy that just come out of the East, Claude was turning out all right," said Rose. "You could see he was the makings of a guy who could do a hell of a job. A lot of people see a cowboy on the TV and they think, boy, I'm going out west to a ranch, and they honestly think they can become a cowboy in a week or a month. That insults the job. Claude didn't have the natural instincts, but he was determined. He wasn't a smart aleck, he didn't let pride get in the way, and he had a hell of a head on his shoulders. He kept his eyes and ears open."

There was much to observe, everything to learn. "They call it the school of hard knocks," said Becky Rose, herself a buckaroo and horsewoman. "You take a lot of ribbing. People laugh at your outfit, laugh at the way you get on and get off, laugh at the way you swing a rope." Dallas endured. He never quite understood horses, never enough to appreciate them as more than a tool, and people remarked that he rode them too hard sometimes and abused them. "But for most of the hammer-headed horses in this country, that's just the way it's done," dismissed Hoyt Wilson. "The horses they give you are five- and

six-year-old nags that they've caught wild and cut at six years
old, and they'll try and kill you if they can." Dallas dominated
the beasts. He coordinated his eastern reflexes to the cow arts.
"Claude finally got the roping down," said Gary Rose. "And
that's tough to learn. You got to handle your horse, you got to
handle your bridle reins, you got to handle your coils, you got
to handle your slack after you throw it, you have to know what
to do with the animal after you got him caught."

The fabled connections were all in his hands . . . the reins,
the rope, guns, the branding iron . . . all he had to do was juggle
them. There was never any doubt that he was physically able.
Hoyt Wilson had seen him scamper up mountainsides lugging
mule loads of post and barbwire on each shoulder. And some
nights he would come riding in at ten o'clock, the wind-chill
factor down to minus twenty degrees, wearing nothing more
than a wet T-shirt. Except for an old Basque who could fish
live coals from a fire with his bare fingers, Hoyt Wilson believed Dallas was "the toughest person mentally I've ever been
around." In the rank and file of other city boys and easterners
who have, since the beginning of cowboy time, showed up "to
ride," Dallas was unique for his discipline. "One year," Rose
remembered, "I was working at the White Horse Ranch and I'll
bet you there was six or eight of them city boys, I mean some
of the most pathetic son of a guns with names like Shenandoah
and Cody. They didn't last a week."

By the following spring, Dallas had begun to look like a
rider, though a distinct one, with a flair for the historical. He
had always stood out for his plain good breeding. He was soft-
spoken and knew better than to sit on clean furniture when he
came off the range. He opened the truck door for ladies, never
smoked or cursed or drank much. When a hand on his way to
the town store took beer orders from the crew, Dallas would

request grapefruit juice or toothpaste or a new toothbrush. He was a fanatic about his teeth . . . never a cavity. He declined to join expeditions to bars and Nevada whorehouses, in part because he had no desire to end up a ravaged old drunk sweeping out the pool hall or riding a little mower tractor around on the owner's ranchhouse lawn. His prudence was also a function of thrift, too. He had some catching up to do on his outfit . . . his saddle, bridles, rope, bedroll, boots, hat, and so on . . . all those things a buckaroo brings with him to the job, some two thousand to three thousand dollars' worth. "When he bought something," said Gary Rose, "he bought the best." His boots were the best, Paul Bonds (a boot custom-made in Nogales, Arizona), three to four hundred dollars, and made to measure. When he bought a blanket, it was top-of-the-line from Eddie Bauer. Moreover, it was obvious that Dallas was starting to develop a certain style. In country proud of its traditions and adherence to the past, he had a taste for things almost more archaic than regional memory could place. He was quiet in his details, never ostentatious, and yet never unaware that, here, it is the details that count. People can tell which valley you come from by the way you roll your pants cuff or tie your "wind rag," or neckerchief, but with Dallas the trick was to know which century he represented. He wore a round-brimmed hat "like something Jim Bridger would wear," a cowhand recalled, almost identical to the Boss of the Plains Raw Edge that J. B. Stetson introduced in 1870. No ordinary bit would do for him either. He hitchhiked three hundred miles to Reno to find the one silversmith who could make a silver-mounted spade bit of a fashion that was discontinued at the turn of the century. "The silversmith said, well I'll make it, but it's going to cost you some money. And Claude said, okay." Besides that centennial .30-30 Winchester, he began to pack a handgun. He wasn't the only buckaroo to carry a firearm. "You might want to shoot a snake with it, you might want to shoot your saddle horse," said Brian Morris, one of the ION region's greatest horsebreakers. "You might want to shoot yourself. If you're down hurt with a horse on top of you and no way out . . . it's happened to people." But in the long memory of Fritz Buckingham, the oldest person in Paradise Valley, Dallas was the only man in many decades who wore a gun just to pick up his mail.

By the spring of 1970, in true buckaroo fashion, Dallas had decided it was time to move on. He wanted to work southward and join one of the larger outfits that still ran a wagon and daily selected mounts from a cavvy of horses. The Alvord Ranch had initiated him to the skills and life-style, but its 53,000 acres had grown too small. Old-style cattle work, sworn to be in its death throes, was rumored to be rawer down south, less adulterated by the present. "Most of those people who were born in Paradise, if you took them to a place like New York or Denver, they'd starve to death before they ever found a restaurant, they're that far behind," said Brian Morris, who then recalled, "I been to Seattle once. That was five minutes in the airport." Dallas was in flight from more than the urban angel, however.

Though he talked very little about it, his draft board was closing in. The ION ranches have long provided sanctuary from outside pressures. Men who have skipped out on their families or gotten sick of paying child support or are running from the law, not infrequently dress themselves in a false background, mutilate their social security cards, and take ranch work. "I've filed probably some hundred or more W-2 forms," said Hoyt Wilson. "There were a lot of strange people on some of our crews, some of them winos, some just strange. And now and then I'd get back inquiries from the government, 'Who the hell is this person?'" Saddle tramps can go for years without detection, then one night they'll get drunk in town, end up in jail, and get identified. Dallas was no ordinary drifter, though. He was young, clean in his habits, eloquent in his tastes. He was different, his voyage into the past clearly charted. The few who knew about his 1-A status did not consider him a draft dodger. "Claude wasn't running from the draft," said Hoyt Wilson, who had served his time with the military. "He didn't look at it that way. He was doing what he was doing. If they caught him, they caught him." All the same, he preferred not to get caught, and so the twenty-year-old boy bought two buck-skins from the Wilsons, "Old Buck" and "Dan," and "he took off out of here with all his gear on one and riding the other." He was going to Canada, he said, but couldn't seem to break away. For the next two months he simply rode through the Steens Range above the Mann Lake Ranch. "About midsummer, he showed up at one of our cabins," said Hoyt Wilson. "He had an old venison haunch strapped across the back of his saddle. No salt, no flour, no nothing. That's all he was surviving on. He spent two weeks with us, then left."

Somewhat later, with Gary and Becky Rose, he found work on the Camel Creek Ranch in central Nevada for a season; and then as the higher federal range closed for the winter, struck off on his own once again, journeying back in time into Paradise Valley. Riding Old Buck and Dan, he headed straight across the desert, sometimes appearing along the interstate highway like a mirage, otherwise lost to the world. He traversed a bleak land teased by the ghosts of water. This was the heart of the Spaniards' Northern Mystery which *conquistadores* had avoided but wistfully furnished with three nonexistent rivers. The northernmost, where Dallas was riding, had been called Rio Buenaventura. Early white voyagers through this desiccated wilderness had bled their mules for soup and eaten insects.

"Everything here seems to declare that, here man shall not dwell," wrote one mountain man. Gold and silver strikes had given men second thoughts, though, and the pockets of hungry miners had brought cattlemen trailing longhorns north from Texas in the late 1860s. Herds were established and, with the help of farmers and sheepherders now subordinate in the local mythology, places like Paradise Valley had flowered . . . flowered with a Spanish accent. The Mexican form of tending cattle had roots on this continent almost three hundred years deeper than the Declaration of Independence. If the great era of the American cowboy, from 1860 to 1890, was father to an institution that colors everything the ION people do and say, then the Mexican *vaquero* was a grandfather.

On horseback, carrying a Winchester and wearing a mountain man's hat, Dallas crossed the mythical Rio Buenaventura, passed the sand dunes of prehistoric Lake Lahontan, and entered a valley where genuine Texas longhorns, the dinosaurs of American cattle, still graze on the precious rangelands even though they don't carry meat like Hereford or Angus do, kept for no other reason than the local ranchers' joy in seeing them. B-52 bombers cruise low over the old forts built to subdue rampaging Bannocks, and a marker remembers the site of the last Indian massacre in history where four Basque herders were mutilated in 1911. A rich vocabulary of Spanish terms that somehow never got anglicized until it was smuggled into the ION region is treated like crown jewels, savored. Buckaroos are considered an endangered species, and old-style fifty-pound bedrolls are preferred over more efficient down sleeping bags because backpacking gear carries Sierra Club connotations. There are ranchers who refuse to use a propane heater for their brands, convinced it and other technology would close the book forever on the cattle industry. And should the cattle industry collapse, they'll tell you, the nation would fold like a soggy card castle. When one newcomer dared to pull down an old apple storage shed on his property, "everybody in the valley raised hell." A telephone hookup can cost upward of $5,600, and that includes the rancher cutting his own cable ditch. Paradise is an island on which change is always expensive and controversial. You surrender to it only when you're down and you've got a horse on top of you and no way out. Hard times that used to be blamed on the sheep industry now get blamed on corporations and the Bureau of Land Management. Though the local preacher still endorses whipping children, that does nothing to keep them on the ranch, and the average age of ranchers has stolen up into the mid-fifties. And so, on that day when a young man appeared out of nowhere on horseback the way their grandfathers had, ready and willing to meet the land on its own brute terms with a hundred-year-old rifle and the ancient vaquero wisdom, no spontaneous conception could have been more legitimate. In short, he was welcome. And Paradise was to be his home for the next ten years.

The first place Dallas stopped was Paradise Hill, which was little more than George Nielsen's roadside bar. There are several strata to Paradise, and as a transplant from California (a "prunie") situated on the very outskirts of the valley beyond a barren stretch known as Paradise Ranchos and mocked as Poverty Flats, Nielsen's bar was ahistorical, even insignificant. When locals said "the bar," what they meant was the J. S. Bar, a congenial, family-oriented saloon eighteen miles deeper into the basin, right at the heart of Paradise Valley, a bar-cum-community center where elementary-school children can buy soft drinks for their lunch and be met by their mothers. Nielsen's place, by contrast, is a dark, meaty boys' club with a poster of a naked woman sectioned like beef and garish whiskey bottle knick-knacks displayed like hoarded sculpture. Of George's bar, one regular warned, "If you don't have your head screwed on tight, you'll get it twisted off by all the lies and bullshit." George Nielsen welcomed the dusty boy like a celebrity, and the two struck up a mutually useful friendship that would last through the next decade. Nielsen would provide a home base, odd jobs, and eventually an outlet for poached furs and meat; Dallas would provide a vicarious ride through the old West from which the aging bar owner was largely excluded.

Returning to Oregon from the Camel Creek Ranch, Gary Rose dropped in at Nielsen's place and found Dallas performing menial jobs around the bar and hungering for real employment on one of the wagon outfits in Paradise. On his behalf, Rose put in a good word with the Morris brothers, each a horsebreaker of wide repute, each working as a buckaroo boss with the large Circle A Ranch. A spot was made for the boy on a seven-man crew. A few days later (after George Nielsen had finished using the celebrity for the time being), Brian Morris sent a truck and horsetrailer up to Paradise Hill and gathered Dallas into the fold. Just as he had divorced himself from Ohio once he reached the Alvord Ranch, Dallas quickly assumed a new distance, this time to his cowboy apprenticeship in Oregon. Few people knew where he'd come from, and he never wrote or phoned the Wilsons on the Alvord Ranch, not until later when he needed their help.

In the springtime and early summer, lupine and yellow sunflowers and Indian paintbrush bloom, spreading color across one mountain so vividly it became known locally as Calico Peak. On all sides the range ripens with native grasses like Idaho fescue, bluebunch wheatgrass, crested wheat, and various forbs and edible weeds like cheatgrass. The cows are moved from winter quarters on the valley floor to the richer and cheaper grazing range "on the mountain." When Dallas was hired on, Circle A buckaroos were caretakers of some nine thousand head, which needed feeding in the winter, calving in the spring, and herding in the summer. Dallas worked hard. During the warmer months, every day was a rodeo (and some Paradise old-timers still pronounce it "rodear," the Spanish verb meaning "to surround or encircle"). Rising long before dawn, at 3:30, the buckaroos would rope a mount from the cavvy of one hundred horses, saddle up, and drive the day's bunch of cattle to the branding trap, usually a space close to camp. Working in pairs, they would rope the head and heels, drop, and brand each unmarked cow or calf. The Bell T, the CM, the Double Square, the Circle A, and so on, each is a show of strength, of property. The history of how and why men scar their animals the way they do is an intricate and telling evidence of empire and delusions of it, endlessly fascinating to the hired men and ranchers alike. Day in and out, the buckaroos reddened brand heads in the superheat of sagebrush fires, seared each cow's left thigh, and with a sharp pocketknife cut wattles on the throat or neck, or notched or slit one ear.

Working for the Circle A, Dallas was befriended by Walt Fischer, an earth- and sun-colored man the size of John Wayne, and his beautiful bride, Irene. The newlyweds ran the cookwagon, which was nothing more than a kitchen mounted onto the back of an army surplus truck, and helped with the branding. Cookwagons are often the province of saddle tramps with bottle fatigue or crippled men who can't get cattle out of their blood. The Fischers were neither. Walt Fischer was one of the finest buckaroos in ION's oral history, and Irene had ridden with outfits on both sides of the law (in the early sixties she got entangled with a gang of rustlers). The quiet boy with little past appealed to them. "I felt he had something deep in him," Irene said. "I thought someday he was going to be famous. He was very intelligent." And besides, "I used to get a big kick out of teasing him and making him blush. Back then you still could. He was just a boy." With the Fischers and Brian Morris and other hands tutoring him, Dallas began to dabble in fading cowboy crafts. "He tried it all," Irene Fischer commented. "And if he didn't like it, if it wasn't good for him, he didn't do it anymore." He learned how to shoe a horse, braid rawhide, reload cartridges, and make his riding gear. His first year he made a pair of spurs, each rowel filed out by hand, and fashioned a pair of woollies, a type of chaps that went out of fashion last century. In every way available, he steeped himself in the artifacts and lore. He devoured Louis L'Amour novels, reading them three and four times. He absorbed the remoteness and space, and took it seriously when Brian Morris asserted in his shorthand lingo that he loved the land because here you can see far, and how a single tree could bring on claustrophobia. At one point he made a pilgrimage to the Charles Russell art museum in Montana, and on returning described it all. He declared that his favorite had to be "A Bronc to Breakfast," in which an early-morning crew not much different from the Circle A bunch is shown being bowled over by a cranky mount.

Never camped far from their cows, they never got fat on the steak and bacon and eggs and flapjack breakfasts and steak and potatoes and hot bread and fruit-pie suppers, nor saw town for months at a time. In Mexico the vaquero was an impoverished mounted laborer, "about as far down in the social order as you could get," according to one chronicler. Here the same destitute proletarian is a national hero, an institution. In 1971

Dallas contributed more than his muscles and impoverishment to the institution, he loaned his face to it when a *National Geographic* photographer named William Albert Allard drove in. The boy was still a rookie, but he was a quick learner and had learned at least to look the part. He even had the cowboy hunker down pat, that utilitarian squat recommended for keeping the bugs, snakes, mud, and dung out of your back pocket. And also, at all times, he packed a gun.

"We were on a trail drive," Allard later recalled, "and came back after I don't know how many days. And that night most of us headed into Winnemucca. Claude rode in with me. We ended up in the Gem Bar, and we were standing side by side, he on my left, closest to the door. And I remember a cop walked in and he walked over and looked at Claude. And he said, 'Hey, you can't wear that in here.' And for the first time I noticed, Claude was still wearing the Colt [Woodsman, a .22 automatic] on his right hip.

"I looked at Claude and I remember the look in his eyes. Very quiet, he didn't say anything, but I thought, oh, this could be a short-fuse situation. And so I spoke right then and there. I said, 'It's no problem, let's go stash it in my truck.' We went out, he took off the holster and belt, wrapped it up, and stuck it under the front seat of the Blazer. We divided ways. I went to take pictures in the whorehouses, he went elsewhere. When I looked, the gun was gone from under the seat."

Dallas was forever practicing with his gun, going through box after box of shells until he was able to keep a tin can in the air. He trained himself to shoot left-handed. With a rifle, he claimed, he could drop an animal a half mile away. Now and then through the summer, he would bring a poached deer or antelope into camp. "We wouldn't need the meat," said Irene Fischer, "and I didn't really want it on the wagon. But I had to accept it. You're not going to waste it. He just never thought about what if the game warden came along out there." No one condemned his poaching any more than they condemned his refusal to give a social security number or pay taxes or answer up to his draft board. Those were his private affairs, and out where there are no walls and no closed doors, the privacy of thoughts is cardinal. After the summer Dallas drifted on to other ranches, because that was the way buckaroos did it. And also because he was wanted.

On September 17, 1970, the federal records state, Claude Dallas, Jr., failed to report for induction to the military. Almost three years later, all the difference between a boy and a man, a grand jury in Columbus, Ohio, indicted him. For the first time in his young life, he was a hunted man. It took a while. The seasons changed. Autumn came and the young buckaroo was sacking out a green colt, breaking it to the feel of a saddle by rubbing a burlap sack over its body. Dallas was no longer a child. He was capable and strong. He had sorted out the fancy and cheap from his schoolboy dream and had turned himself into a good, working Nevada cowboy, shy of trees, filled with the patois, and self-contained. Tell him to do a job, and you knew it would get done. No one would catch him posing dramatically with a rifle in the crook of his arms anymore, and he knew enough to remove his handgun around a bucking colt. When three men dressed like cowboys approached the corral, he may have dismissed them as dudes for their costumes; he may have been too preoccupied to notice. Either way, they were between him and his gun when the sky caved in and he was toppled further than any dreamer should have to fall. They handcuffed him. They read him his rights. He was under arrest. Years later he would claim they had not even given him time to arrange feed or water for the colt. They just dragged him off to Ohio dressed the way he'd always hoped to be.

Claude Dallas's senior photograph in the Mount Gilead High School yearbook. "As soon as he graduated, he was going to the Rocky Mountains," said a classmate. "He had that dream from the start. He wanted to get established as a mountain man."

In the spring of 1969, Dallas asked an Oregon rancher if he could become a buckaroo. "So we did it," said the rancher. "We took him out riding."

A beer break at a Circle A line camp. On the right, Dallas is wearing chinks (short fringed chaps), distinct from the lime-green sheepskin "woollies" he is wearing in the previous photo.

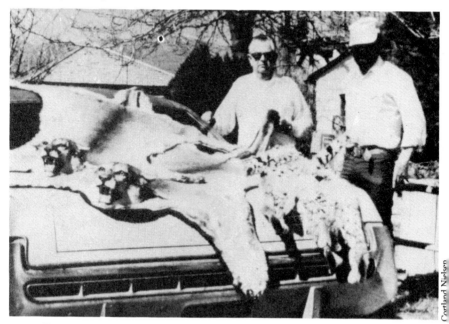

Disenchanted with buckarooing, Dallas branched off into trapping. Here, with his friend George Nielsen, he displays two cougar skins and several bobcat pelts.

With his best friend Jerry Thiessen, Bill Pogue (*left*) enjoys a campfire in one of the Owyhee's many canyons. "Bill told me a number of times, somebody's going to get killed," said Thiessen. "He knew there were people out there who could do it and that sooner or later it was going to happen." It happened to him. Once the gunsmoke cleared, the second victim, Conley Elms (*inset*), became trivial in the spreading tales of Bull Camp.

David Brookman/Idaho Statesman

In front of this sheepherder's tent, Dallas drew from his holster and gunned down the two game wardens, then shot each behind the ear, trapper-style.

David Brookman/Idaho Statesman

Sheriff's Investigator
Stan Rorex (left)
and Humboldt County
Sheriff Frank Weston (right)
examine traps left by Dallas.

# Chapter 4

*T*WO thousand miles long, the outrage stretched. They hauled him cross-country in a car, berthing him in drunk tanks at the end of each driving day. "He hated that," said one friend. "Any sort of enclosure was bad, of course, but getting thrown in with drunks and perverts was terrible for him. At the time he wasn't a high security risk, though. He didn't rate different dwellings." The journey was a long extended chain of insults. By the time he reached Columbus, Ohio, the abuse was complete. "Those son of a bitches had taken his boots off," said his father, "and knocked the heels off." Claude Dallas, Sr., was waiting with the five-hundred-dollar bail bond at the Federal Building when he first saw his son. "This marshal, big overgrown bastard like most of them are, he comes in with that boy of mine weighing about a hundred sixty-five, and he didn't have a coat to his name. They dragged him all the way back in his cowboy clothes. He had a shirt and no undershirt and it was raining and freezing, and they brought him there wet to the skin and colder than hell, belly handcuffed. They'd walked him down the street six or seven blocks like that. And I told that big potgut, 'It must take a hell of a man to drag a kid like that down the street.'" Bond was immediately posted, and father and son retreated to a motel where the boy changed clothes. "And then we went out and I bought him a steak dinner."

Dallas had been arrested on October 15. He was released to his father eleven days later, and trial was slated for January 8, 1974. His attorney, Andrew Wentworth, scrambled to find a loophole. There was no question that Dallas had received notice to appear from his draft board and had defied it. That was a felony violation for which he now faced two years of alternative service in a hospital or institution, or nine to thirteen months in a federal penitentiary. As is standard when dealing with the U.S. Attorney's office, the defense was handed the entire file of documents that pertained to the trial. The FBI forwarded a four-inch stack of records, including regulations and correspondence from the draft board in Mount Gilead. For Wentworth the case was unusual. "I liked him very much, there was an independent air about him. You think of a cowboy coming in with a hat all the time. Dallas came in with blue jeans, a clean white work shirt, and no hat. You think of them way out west never taking their hats off. They darn near have their spurs on while they do the Texas two-step or something. He wasn't like that. He just presented himself as a plain, hardworking guy.

"The thing that was remarkable about the case was that most of the draft cases you saw were guys who just didn't want to go. They didn't like the Vietnam War, they didn't want to serve in the army, they didn't want the discipline. Dallas wasn't that kind of a guy. He wasn't a protestor. He was an individualist. He was probably born two hundred years too late. His problem was that he didn't want anybody telling him what to do. He reminded me of Jeremiah Johnson and in other respects he reminded me of Kirk Douglas in *Lonely Are the Brave* [based on *The Brave Cowboy* by Edward Abbey]. He sort of epitomized that feeling. I never met anybody before or since that was like him. Of course, how many cowboys do you run into in Columbus, Ohio?"

The case was unusual, too, in that the Selective Service was on the verge of being phased out and, elsewhere, draft evasion cases were taking low spot on federal prosecutors' agendas. "I would say that we were at the end of the continuum nationally," Wentworth observed. "Draft dodger cases had peaked long before in other parts of the country. But we were still prosecuting them here." Wentworth hired two law clerks to pore through the file, and after three weeks they discovered a small discrepancy. The Mount Gilead draft board had never indicted anyone until after a second notice to appear had been served. Dallas had received his first notice, but no one on the draft board could prove that he had received a second notice. It was a niggling point and technically Dallas was guilty of failure to appear, but Wentworth recognized it as the loophole he had been hired to find. It was, he felt, enough to produce a reasonable doubt in the minds of the jury. Not only was the government still prosecuting draft cases in Ohio even as the President was abolishing the draft, but it was singling out a hardworking cowboy for punishment, treating him one way and everybody else differently. Here was no hippie radical throwing bottles of blood on draft records. Here was the backbone of the nation.

He was neat, his hair was short, and his heart was free. He brands the hamburgers you eat, ladies and gentlemen of the jury, rides herd on the dreams you sleep with. The U. S. Attorney apparently agreed. One day before trial, the charges were dropped and Dallas was free to go. It was no occasion for joy. The law had hunted him, handcuffed him, torn the heels from his boots, and sweated him and his family up to the last possible minute. And as he was boarding a bus to return to Nevada, he later told a friend, an FBI agent showed up to stick a thorn in his pocket. "I'll get you, Claude," said the agent. "I'll get you even if it's for tax evasion."

He had borrowed money from his first ION employers, the Wilsons, to help pay for his defense, and he took his debts seriously. "He called me," said Hoyt Wilson. "He said he was free and when did I want him out to work off the money he owed. I said, be here the first of May to move the cattle up the mountain. I went to Burns for supplies on the thirtieth and got back around five. And there he was, coming over the ridge, packing one horse, riding the other. He'd ridden [260 miles] up from Fallon." It was his familiar entrance, but he was different. "He'd changed," said Wilson. "He came back more savvy, more wary. He had felt the heat of authority and he didn't enjoy it." Dallas was back in the saddle, but either he'd grown or the saddle had shrunk or both. "In my opinion," he would declare later, "the cow outfits were going to hell." After a month or so, with his debt to the Wilsons cleared, he took off for Paradise.

Gone from the ION region for less than a year, he returned to Paradise to find cowmen everywhere dazed and aghast like hornets smoked from their nest. Fresh from his own scrape with the feds, Dallas rode horseback into a landscape suddenly plagued with strange, life-sucking federal acronyms that promised disaster for the ranchers and death to the working cowboy.

For years federal legislation had been stacking up against them, but no one had paid much attention. The laws had not always been unfriendly. Indeed, back in 1934 cattlemen had taken good advantage of the Taylor Grazing Act (which established the legal rights of livestock grazing on public land) to shut down most of the competing sheep operations. Along with the act came a steward agency called the Grazing Service, a passive, procattle body that did little more than collect the rent on grazing privileges, a flat five cents per AUM (or Animal Unit Month; much of the Paradise area is known as "twenty- or thirty-acre country" because it takes twenty to thirty acres of forage to produce one AUM). The fee increased after World War II when the Grazing Service was melded into the General Land Office (in 1946) to form the Bureau of Land Management, but still remained so low that it actually served as a government subsidy to the cattle industry. Cattle was so firmly king that wags dubbed the BLM the Bureau of Livestock and Mining.

No one really took notice when the Multiple Use and Classification Act was passed in 1964, introducing the wild notion of "multiple use" of public lands. Nor were the grumbles particularly loud when the National Environmental Policy Act (NEPA) of 1969 brought to federal vocabulary the Environmental Impact Study (EIS). NEPA, EISs, Multiple Use: they were watery Washington brews, and out west, reality remained as it always had been, coffee a horseshoe would float in. In 1973, though . . . the same year Claude Dallas was yanked from his horsebreaking by the FBI . . . the cow industry suddenly found itself choking on a vision of the future filled with bureaus, acts, agents, regulations, and strange ideas. In that year the National Resources Defense Council (NRDC) and five other environmental groups challenged in U.S. District

Court the BLM's national grazing program. The BLM was re-
buked and ordered to prepare 212 extensively detailed EISs on
its holdings (fourteen in Nevada) on a site-by-site basis by
1988. Ranchers reeled. For until an EIS was prepared on the
BLM's grazing ranges, the construction of new fences, corrals,
and water troughs and the drilling of new wells were all frozen.
In the coming years, things got even worse. The EISs began to
show how dominant the livestock programs had been on federal lands, to the exclusion of other uses. The Federal Land
Policy and Management Act (FLPMA) of 1976 directed that
federal lands be preserved in their natural condition "to provide
food and habitat for fish and wildlife and domestic animals and
provide for outdoor recreation, human occupancy and use." As
if that weren't bad enough, the act further proclaimed that public lands would not be given back to the states. And the crown-
ing farce came when the U.S. Supreme Court ruled that a
subterranean mutant, the Devil's Hole pupfish, had prior rights
to the very water their cows needed. What this all meant in real
terms was that the clock was going to be pushed back; the
cattle range was going to be systematically dismantled for a
"native range."

The nation hungered for beef, and the cowboy had always
delivered. The nation hungered for ritual, and the cowboy had
answered again. Without them, said one ION rancher, "why,
the country would starve to death in short order." But starting
around the time Dallas rode back into Paradise after his own
tangle with the feds, what the cattlemen got in return for their
spine-busting labors was a prolonged castration. BLM agents
had traditionally been good old boys prone to wearing tooled
boots and inlaid silver belt buckles, and to jawboning with the
ranchers. All that changed in the 1970s. The ten-man BLM
office in Winnemucca turned into an army of two hundred

geologists, economists, soil scientists, range conservationists, recreation specialists, wildlife biologists, archaeologists, and support personnel, all in search of that abstract Eldorado called "multiple use." Tales were told about their feverish quest.

One morning, for instance, a college girl hired by the BLM wandered on to a rancher's private land and, while he watched from his house, took measurements and remeasurements. Finally she drove up to introduce herself and deliver some disturbing information. His well was in the wrong place. Also, she announced, his fence was set in wrong sections. In fact, according to her map, some of his fence didn't even exist. The rancher took it all in, cogitated for a somber moment, and then very helpfully pointed out that she had the wrong map and was on the wrong land. Another rancher drilling a water well for his cattle hit a table of obsidian six hundred feet down, and soon had glassy, black debris piled all around his hole. Before long, an agent drove up and, sure enough, halted the drilling, insisting that the obsidian debris was an archaeological arrowhead find. ION folk culled dozens of such jackass stories from their confrontations with the BLM. But while the jokes were funny, the situation definitely was not, and throughout the West, federal employees found themselves insulted, locked off bureau land, and periodically confronted by ranchers brandishing rifles. Hatred of the bureau grew to such proportions that the state of Nevada tried to promote better feelings by offering a cash prize in a "Rename the BLM" contest. Any vehicle with government-stenciled letters on the door, Department of the Interior or not, was suspect. Census takers were accused of spying for the BLM or being agents in disguise. And on the ranchers' behalf, the Reverend Laverne Inzer opined that the BLM was an immoral organization.

Fritz Buckingham, a denizen of Paradise Valley for eight

decades, could remember when the sagebrush range had been covered with bunchgrass that grew as high as your stirrups. That was an earlier age, though, one that few alive had ever seen and which many preferred to disbelieve. To the charges that shortsighted cattle barons ("Baron?" snapped one rancher. "I don't know what you mean by the term 'baron'") had over-grazed the range to the point of devastation, each rancher re-peated verbatim the same wounded defense: "I don't abuse the land. I can't. It's my livelihood, damn it. I'd only be abusing myself." What they called grass, though, most often was cheat-grass, a European weed that had taken over the range at the beginning of the century. The BLM and Forest Service said it had no forage value. From the definition of what was grass, to the reductions of grazing allotments, halts to fencing and drill-ing, and requirements that cattle on public lands be ear-tagged (with plastic, color-coded tags numbered for record keeping), ranching was being changed. The feds had become strict, fero-cious sticklers for the written rule, and that was costing ranch-ers a lot of money.

While tending some pivot sprinklers for a rancher one day, Dallas was paid a visit by a BLM agent who drove out to evict him from a piece of public ground. "He was camped on BLM property," said Harold Chapin, a mustanger. "It was either camp there outside the fence or underneath the sprinklers, he didn't have a hell of a lot of choice. And with dust as deep as your knees what could the man hurt with his tent and his bed setting?" It was typical, though. The Environmental Pro-tection Agency showed up to slap ranchers and farmers with pollution-control laws when their plows raised huge clouds of spring dust, and the Office of Safety and Health Administra-tion brought in safety standards. Cattlemen were even told they couldn't butcher their own cows without government-certified conditions. Plagued by the BLM, EPA, OSHA, NRDC, NEPA, and other acronyms, the ranchers came up with an acronym of their own, LASER (League for the Advancement of Equal Rights), composed of ranchers who used federal lands. Paradise was in revolution, almost literally. Representing nearby Elko County in the Nevada state assembly, a rancher named Dean Rhoads introduced the so-called Sagebrush Rebellion bill in 1979 in an attempt to appropriate for the state some forty-nine million acres of public lands. Among many others, the next President of the United States, Ronald Reagan, declared himself a Sagebrush Rebel, too.

More than government regulations were changing the cattle industry in the 1970s, however. Technology was sharpshooting the ION cowboy from his center-fire saddle in alarming numbers. Since Genesis, it seemed, cowboys had trailed their herds on horseback. Then the truck invaded northern Nevada, the stronghold of cowboy antiquity. In the early seventies, when big semis began to take over the transport of cattle from winter quarters to the summer range on the mountain, said one Paradise local, "We laughed uproariously at them." But the trucks proved out. Smaller pickup trucks, which had already proved their starch, took on an expanded capability with the introduction of the gooseneck trailer. With the combination of pickup and trailer, you could load your horse on at 6:00 A.M. and show up at the branding trap a day's horseback ride away by 7:00 . . . and be back home by suppertime. Thus mobilized, the buckaroo no longer had to sleep in a tent for five months of the year with cavvies of mounts and a laboriously supplied cookwagon. In the winter he didn't have to live near a hay camp; machines now produced hay bales that could be tossed in a truck bed, driven to a herd, cut, and kicked off the tailgate. And you could still catch the Sunday afternoon ball game in color. Irrigation dams using canvas were updated with fiberglass, and gigantic pivot sprinklers that dispensed sixteen hundred gallons of water per minute began to appear in the middle of two-hundred-acre circles of greenery. Despite community reluctance (which ignored evidence that old, saturated septic tanks may have contributed to a killing outbreak of typhoid fever in the twenties), a sewer system was installed in Paradise Valley. In the seventies, too, the one-channel TV reception blossomed with four more stations, including one from Chicago, and that had a dramatic effect on the children, who no longer talked about becoming buckaroos (in fact, they quit using the term because of its association with drudgery). "In the westerns," commented Frankie Zabala, a pretty schoolteacher at the town's elementary school, "the horses are always saddled. You gallop as fast as you can and your horse never gets tired. You're never dirty. All the ranchers end up millionaires." And they're called cowboys, never buckaroos.

"It's definitely the foreigners who bring in technology," said Zabala. "And the locals rebel against it as long as they can." The gooseneck trailer, the pivot sprinkler, the semi truck, and television all became part of the rancher's life. Other advances didn't. Vaccines, for instance, are generally not used unless absolutely required or an epidemic threatens. "The attitude is, if it was good enough without vaccine in Gramp's day, it's good enough now," remarked Liz Chabot, the town's justice of the peace, schoolbus driver, and vaccine saleswoman, probably Paradise's most lively citizen. "If the cow's going to get sick and die, it's her own fault. Some ranches will buy *some* vaccine. But I don't push it. The minute you push it, they won't buy. That's the way people are around here. Ranching is way behind and they're stubborn." They were stubborn, too, about artificial insemination, pregnancy tests, ear-tagging, and herd books

(which record the life of each cow from birth to slaughter-
house). Many preferred to recognize problems in their cattle
after they had occurred. Individual cows would be distin-
guished by the markings on their faces, or because they were
chronically troublesome or odd. Pregnancy or a missing calf
was recognized by a tight "bag," or udder. The ranchers were
obstinate in their refusal to accept more cost-effective methods,
and the irony was that while, in Sheriff Tim Nettleton's opinion, "you've probably got some of the toughest businessmen in
the world down there, if there's something to be had, they'll
jump on it," still they refused to make cow production safer or
less expensive. Most symbolic of the resistance to new ways
was Paradise Valley ranchers' continuing refusal to use a
squeeze chute. A squeeze chute is basically a giant metal trap.
Channeled single file down a stock chute, each cow enters the
contraption individually, a lever is pressed down, and the cow
is immobilized with its head and neck sticking through a collar-
hole. Working with his teenage son or daughter, a rancher can
brand, ear-tag, castrate or spay, vaccinate, and administer a
growth implant in as many as fifty cows in three hours. It takes
eight to twelve cowboys . . . four or six on horseback . . . to
accomplish the same task buckaroo-style. The bottom line to
objections lay in a remark made by Les Stewart, the widely
respected owner of the 96 Ranch. "If we can't run a cow ranch
the way a cow ranch ought to be run," he flatly stated, "then
we'll quit." And he meant it. He continues to use the same
stacked willow-branch corral his grandfather built, and, aptly
enough, is the proud owner of Marlboro, the Texas longhorn
pictured in famous cigarette ads.

The community has practically a religious faith in family-
raised, grass-fed beef. Ranchers will admit frankly that if it
weren't for an enterprising grandfather who homesteaded or

purchased or simply squatted on the land way back when, they would have gone belly up in today's inflation-choked marketplace. What you don't hear much of is that it doesn't much matter, one way or the other, if they ranch or not. As Oregon writer William Boly pointed out in a critical article, "In the grand scheme of things, the Marlboro man doesn't raise many cattle. In fact, Public Lands produce enough forage for only about 4 percent of the nation's cattle, which happens to be less than the annual variation in America's collective appetite for beef. The real cattle-raising states—Nebraska, Missouri, Kansas, Iowa—do so in feedlots." In 1979 Nevada ranked even with Vermont in annual beef production, a mortifying thirty-seventh in the nation. As if that weren't humbling enough, a range scientist informed Boly that "a Mississippi black in overalls isn't as photogenic as a cowboy with his pony. But he's sure as hell a lot more efficient at raising beef." Buckarooing was in a rout.

When Dallas first worked on the Circle A Ranch, it had carried nine thousand head. With the breakup of centralized ranching into leased portions, a mere thousand head became a large herd, and several ranches carried as few as two hundred to three hundred. Not only were crews of six and eight professional buckaroos an impossible expense on outfits that small, they were unnecessary. What few buckaroos remained had to violate the caballero's one golden rule . . . that dignity rides in a saddle . . . and shoulder other types of ranch labor such as haying, irrigating, and well drilling. The cowboy was being killed off. Everyone said so. By the late seventies there simply were no more full-time mounted buckaroos. Those who, like Brian Morris, had a genius for handling horses and cows, drifted on to other outfits in the ION region, searching out work men had forgotten how to do (even if it meant working for the BLM). Walt Fischer moved to Idaho with his wife, Irene, in search of construction work or a job driving trucks, and ended up employed by a race track in Dubois. After seven months, the Fischers returned to Paradise Valley and took on the hybrid ranch work that was only part-time riding. They worked on the Flat Creek Ranch until 1978, when an early-morning mount "blew up" and tried to kill Walt Fischer (just like the bucking horse in "A Bronc to Breakfast," Claude's favorite Russell painting).

It was the last day of a small drive from the mountain to a valley ranch, and except for one young boy and Walt Fischer, the crew had already departed with the cattle. The mean-spirited horse dove into a willow thicket and finally managed to rid itself of the rider. Fischer was thrown hard. Half his rib cage was separated from his spine, one lung was punctured, and he was knocked unconscious. Terrified, the boy tried unsuccessfully to start the pickup in camp, then gave up and caught another horse, saddled it, and rode for help seventeen miles away. During the long day, Fischer revived, crawled to the dead pickup, and tried to pull himself up into the cab, but ended up back in the dirt. Not until dusk did they find the rangy man. It was nine o'clock before a truck bore him down from Martin Creek. An ambulance sped the dying cowboy to Winnemucca, and then on to Reno. There, after eighteen hours and two hundred miles of agony, his heart stopped. "He went out," said Irene Fischer. "They put fibrillators on him. They punched a hole in him and blew his lung back out." And the cowboy lived again. "What hurt him worse than that horse, though," she remembered, "was that he'd put fifteen years into the Circle A. And the manager fired him because he got thrown. Just like an old horse. Shoot him, don't even put him out to pasture."

★   ★   ★

Dallas adapted to the overthrow of the working cowboy in Paradise Valley, but with a difference, with his special talent for anachronism. The past, the wilderness, the candle flame of adventure . . . once again he carefully braided them into the rope of fantasies he had begun as a child. He had voyaged backward a hundred years to arrive at Paradise Valley. Now he traveled back another fifty to a time so distant it must have seemed an unbreachable sanctuary. During the warmer months, he hayed like a common farmer, irrigated, built fence, drilled water wells, drove tractors on the potato farms, and jockeyed semis through northern Nevada. He shoed horses and butchered cows. When the opportunity arose, he would buckaroo . . . riding, roping, branding. The choreography was no longer simple, though; it was diverse and adulterated. The work he took, when and where he wanted, was of a type no self-respecting buckaroo would have considered ten years earlier. But he performed it and well, making his wages, living in a tent near the job or in a trailer behind George Nielsen's bar. He impressed women with his good manners and men with his sturdy, good labor. Cow country was in an uproar. Technology and the feds had nailed the cowboy's coffin shut before he'd even quit convulsing. But Dallas was calm, for he had a secret winter life.

When the temperatures dropped and the horses turned shaggy and the nights long, it was trapping season. Since 1971 or so, Dallas had been trapping coyotes and bobcats on a recreational scale. "Ninety percent enjoyment, ten percent profit," according to a close friend. "Then in 1976 it reversed, ten percent enjoyment, ninety percent profit." The fur trade had always been a boom-bust economy. When silk replaced beaver felt in the 1800s, mountain men turned to harvesting buffalo for meat, furs, and tongues. In the twentieth century, short-haired furbearers like mink, beaver, and muskrat became popular again, particularly in the 1940s and 1950s. Their value dropped once more, then regained some popularity in the 1970s, and leveled off at around twelve dollars per beaver pelt. At the same time, something remarkable happened to the virtually worthless long-haired furs from coyotes, bobcats, foxes, and raccoons. "Previously you couldn't give them away," said Neil Johnson, a fur specialist with Idaho Fish and Game. "If you were lucky you could get fifty cents for the pelt, a dollar fifty for the ears as a bounty in a lot of states." No one liked the coyote. Ranchers saw their calves devoured alive as they emerged from the womb, and found still living cows that had lost their entire rumps to a pack. In Humboldt County, a Basque named Santy Mendietta was hired by the government to trap and shoot, and (from 1948 to 1972) to dispense the infamous poison 1080 in an effort to reduce their numbers. Then, in the mid-1970s, European fur tastes unexpectedly came to the rescue. The price of a coyote pelt rose over a hundredfold. In 1978–79, the boom year, a 50¢ coyote with $1.50 ears became worth $60. Bobcats fetched over $280. Suddenly every farmer's son was out with his number 3 Victors trapping the back forty and, inevitably, laming the neighbor's dogs. The surge in trapping was the best thing ranchers could have wished for, better even than 1080, which worked like black magic but killed half the food chain to boot.

Professional trappers like Santy Mendietta and Ken Klaumann ran "long lines" of three hundred to five hundred traps that were buried and baited close to the desert roads, where they could more easily be checked by vehicle in three- to five-day circles. Claude Dallas was different. His lines were short, consisting of no more than eighty sets, and he tended them on

foot. He was inexperienced, and the craft took him even longer
to acquire than cowboying. "I don't think Dallas was a good
trapper," said Mendietta, who had caught some hundred thousand animals in his day. "The man worked hard, but he didn't
catch too many. I think he would have made a hell of a trapper,
but he was starting from scratch and he needed somebody to
show him how." Where the beginning cowboy's is a school of
hard knocks, the novice trapper enters a cloister of trial, error,
and silence. You can't learn by example from a half dozen others on the crew because there is no crew. You can't really practice, and instruction is mainly self-taught. Alone, you have to
become fluent in sign, a scholar of coyote or bobcat logic. To
break even on your expenses (a dozen traps cost sixty dollars),
you must calculate how a creature can best be seduced (Klaumann claims coyote heads and musk-ox urine are the bait to
use), how to make a buried set odorless as well as invisible
(some boil their new traps, gloves, and shoes with sagebrush,
some just throw new traps in the river to rust, which works out
the telltale oil smell), and whether to leave one, two, or three
sets at a site and whether to stake the sets down or weight them
with rock drags (which prevent the animal from breaking off its
foot in cold weather and escaping, but which also entails chasing the animal through the bush). Beginners can take more
than thirty minutes to set a trap. Faced with setting a hundred
traps a day, the professional can spend only three or four minutes with each. Once the animal is caught, you need to know
how to kill it, how to skin it quickly (three to five minutes for
the professional—"It's like taking off your underwear," said
Klaumann), how to stretch the pelt, and when to turn the drying pelt right side out again. At season's end you need to know
how good the quality of your furs really is (buyers prize white
and light-colored coyote pelts because they can be spotted ar-

tificially with dye and passed off as lynx), how much to hold out for, and if and when to sell. No one helped Dallas. He didn't ask much; no one volunteered much. For one thing trappers are every bit as territorial as the animals they harvest. Unlike hunters who migrate from area to area different years, each trapper has and keeps a clearly defined, mental map of what territory belongs to whom, and a quick instinct for trespassers. Trappers maintain a hairtrigger fraternity, united against critics of the steel trap, but essentially selfish and paranoid ("Touch My Trap," warns one bumper sticker, "I'll Break Your Face"). When it comes to sales at fur auctions, the dealings and brokerage are cutthroat and Byzantine, fraught with brokers trying to outbuy, corner, or simply sink the local market. Prices fluctuate dizzily from one year to the next, one town to another, and each trapper is looking to his own best interests while there's still a market worth trapping for.

Dallas wound his way slowly into the tangled world of trapping, experimenting in the Bloody Run Hills above Paradise Hill, where he kept his possessions, and finally branching out into central Nevada and the Owyhee Desert. It was a crude, basic sort of life, far less comfortable than cowboying, but also less encumbered. There was no one at all telling him what to do for two months at a time while the furs were prime and every rare word was a puff of frost. He was his own boss, his own teacher. The nature of his work—fur trapping with at most a horse for daily transport, alone beneath the storms with his rifle and gun—harked back to the most primitive of American frontiers. "Claude felt that when he was out there in the wilderness, he was pretty much a law unto himself," a friend recalled.

One winter his brother Bob visited and found a mountain man living primitively in a cave at Castle Rock on the South

Fork of the Little Humboldt. Claude had covered poles with dirt, plastic, and a second layer of dirt, and furnished the dugout with a potbellied stove. The dwelling overlooked a meadow that provided hay for his two horses. When the forage ran out, he simply turned the horses loose to fend for themselves and picked them up later in the spring. Across the meadow some hundred yards was a hillside on which he set up targets. "He could lie beside his potbellied stove all day long," said Hoyt Wilson, "and sight in his rifle, cast bullets, load them up, and never have to go outside." With one of the rifles, a muzzle-loaded .50 caliber Sharps buffalo gun, he claimed to have knocked down a wild horse at eight hundred yards. The Wild Horse Act of 1971 had brought horses under federal protection (article 1 read: "Wild, free-roaming horses and burros are living symbols of the historic and pioneer spirit of the West"), and there was a stiff thousand-dollar fine for killing one. But Dallas didn't care.

"I seen Claude one day," said Klaumann. "He said, 'Come here, me and my brother finally got some meat.' He said, 'Here, take a chunk off.' And he cut me a big steak. I brought it home and chucked it in the freezer. Later Mom cooked it up. It was sweet and tasted different. And I got to thinking, ah shit, I know damn well that was a piece of horse." Far from objecting to Dallas's subsistence on a living symbol of the West, the locals generally approved. "At one time people were proud to have a few head of wild horses on their place, the western mystique and all that," explained Gary Thrasher of the Nevada First Corporation (which owned the Circle A Ranch). "But then the wild horses went berserk. Numbers on the Owyhee where Nevada First had grazing permits jumped from three hundred in 1970 to two thousand by 1983. And technically these horses belonged to Nevada First because they were on our grazing land, and we got fined a trespassing fee, which was double the grazing fee for twelve months. Now wild horses are no better than rodents." Horses have no natural predator except for man, and it was man, in the guise of mustangers, who had always controlled their population. The progeny of old and escaped cowboy and cavalry mounts, the herds had long been trimmed by mustangers, who made a business of selling the finest horses to ranches for their cavvies, and the rest to chicken-feed, fertilizer, and dogfood companies. When the Wild Horse Act halted the trade, the effect in Paradise was further headshaking and anger at the "educated idiots" from Washington. "They took my living from me," said Harold Chapin, a former mustanger who saw the act as an affront to intelligence and capitalism. "The problem with the government is that they got no common sense. At least when they had private people runnin' those horses they had tax money comin' in instead of tax money goin' out. It's ridiculous." As Gary Thrasher put it, "The mustang got to be a symbol of government interference." Carefree, old-fashioned, and living his life like a ballad, Dallas asked no one permission, certainly not the feds, when he journeyed out to shoot wild horses for meat and trap bait.

All winter long the Dallas brothers roughed it at Castle Rock. Claude ran his trapline while Bob worked for a rancher feeding cattle hay. Everywhere the brothers went was on foot. One day, people still recall, one of the Dallas boys walked thirty miles round trip for a candy bar. They were unabashedly pedestrians, walking, not riding, not driving, among the outcrops of a mountain man's fantasy. There are rumors that they cached thirty pounds of gunpowder with other supplies in the region. At the end of the winter . . . just as other Dallas brothers had . . . Bob disengaged from the raw dream. "My four youngest boys went out there to be with Claude at different times," said their father. "But then they saw how hard it is. That isn't an easy life. And none of them took it up." But Claude stuck with it, the cave, the muzzle-loader, the primitivism. He believed in the persona. One day he brought five freshly poached deer hides to Irene Fischer and asked her to tan them and make a buckskin outfit for him. (She didn't, concerned she might get caught with the illegal hides.) During part of one winter, it was said, he lived with a woman. Presumably the experience was too rugged for her, which only strengthened Dallas's belief that women were a burden in the wilderness.

"You know they write those stories glorifying how men went out one fall and camped in some canyon and built them a cabin and caught five otter and six muskrats and some deer and cats, whatever," rhapsodizes Santy Mendietta, sixty years old with a physique half that old and a dog named Zorro, so ugly it doesn't just chase cars, it bites the tires. For what it's worth, Mendietta can pinpoint the most obscure drift fence in the Owyhee, but is totally befuddled when asked where the county courthouse (five blocks away) is. He is a minor legend, a tough, wry man who is nevertheless just as glad to have transcended the cold camps and wilderness days. "Hell, can you imagine a man going through all that?" he asks. "No. If I had to go out and catch my furs on snowshoes, I couldn't even afford to buy salt and pepper. No, I'll leave them guys be wherever they might be, the old-timers."

Dallas thrived on the hardships, though. He could have blunted the harshness of his winterings and multiplied his profits by running a long line by truck and camper like Mendietta and Klaumann. But, except for a large canvas sheepherder's tent that eventually replaced his Castle Rock dugout, he largely spurned civilization's ease. He welcomed the past as a sort of monasticism, a geography of discomforts and solitude fed by wild mustang meat. "The hunter is essentially a lonely man," he had read as a boy. He was alone, but never really. Everyone in Paradise knew who Claude Dallas was and had a rough idea of how to find him. It was a small community, and the young man touched a nerve in many of them. Men who refused the tools and techniques of modern ranching could not help but notice that the archaic was working for Dallas, too. He lived like them, he looked like them (or their ancestors), he talked like them. He took his daily meat with a rifle. Something about him . . . his habit of obscuring his origins perhaps, or his quietness and Gary Cooper manners . . . appealed to many of the local women especially. There was an element of the orphan in him, which brought their maternal instincts to the surface like pools of sweet water. Half a dozen women or more considered him a son (their own sons were gone from Paradise to the mines or city construction crews or agriculture colleges, gone from the valley), and he was always welcome for dinner. Liz Nielsen would claim later he was dearer than her own stepson.

In another way, too, Dallas was not alone. For he had a financial partner. It remains unclear just when George Nielsen began grubstaking the trapper, but an arrangement developed in which Dallas was regularly provided with groceries, gear, horses, transportation into and out of the desert, the delivery of mail and messages, and a ready, cash-on-the-pelt market . . . for 40 percent of the take. Dallas had rarely (if ever) given an employer his social security number, rarely (if ever) paid taxes, and only observed game laws when it suited him. He purchased trapping licenses, but persistently viewed the desert and mountains as separate from regulation. He went to great lengths to avoid the red tape of accounting for pelts. Once he approached Reverend Inzer with one hundred dollars if he would sell some of his furs. Inzer did, and considered the payment generous until it was pointed out that the capital gain would show in his name, not Claude's. The trapper regularly poached deer for his own consumption, to use as trap bait, and to turn over to George Nielsen, who then sold it to wetbacks on the local farms (again for a 40 percent cut). People told of Nielsen opening his freezer and inadvertently exposing fresh venison quarters in midsummer. The partnership was not only a source of extra income, it also provided Nielsen with a share in the rugged life-style. Possibly because he sensed that desire to identify, Dallas called his benefactor a "leppy son of a bitch," a mixture of affection and insult. When a calf loses its mother and wanders about bawling aimlessly, it's known in ION lingo as a leppy.

The Paradise Hill bar's personality was rough and Nielsen cultivated its dingy, outlaw spirit. Detractors described it as a cesspool, and even the patrons would tell tales of how stolen horsetrailers, guns, and other hot property were fenced there, of parties in which the bar was closed and prostitutes imported from the Line in Winnemucca for extended orgies, and of the sale of drugs. ("Any good bar's got those things, though," Sheriff Nettleton observed with a grin.) With the mounting tension between the government and ranchers, talk was loose and loud in Nielsen's bar about doing violence to BLM agents. When Bristlewolf killed three people with a shotgun, it was reasoned the hermit must have thought they were feds. During a discussion about purchasing a rifle, someone remarked that unless you hunted there was no need to own one, and Dallas responded, "You can always go out and shoot a BLM man." It may have sounded like a joke, but he is said later to have plotted a bank robbery. When asked what an appropriate response might be if a guard appeared, Dallas replied, "Kill him." These statements were extraordinary, though, because Dallas actually had to utter them. Ordinarily he had George Nielsen to say them for him. "George is the type of guy who would say, 'I'll shoot the so and so,'" said one Paradise resident. "But he's not the type of guy who will go and do it. He hates the law, and if there's any way for him to embarrass the law he'll do it. But he wouldn't actually kill a lawman." Nielsen was a loud, aging alcoholic, heavy on the invective and spitemongering, and he loved to brag about the raw menace of his young mountain man. He boasted of Dallas's ever-present handgun . ... on the hip, in a shoulder holster, or tucked in a boot holster as a "hideout." No one needed reminding. They all knew that Dallas collected and traded weapons, but so did a lot of people. He was befriended by an investigator for Nevada Motor Carriers, named Duane Michelson, who would join the trapper in back of the bar for an hour or two of makeshift pistol practice every now and then. Dallas was fascinated with police marksmanship, technique, and "combat" shooting, a glorified form of target practice which stressed speed and the ability to shoot without lining up the target in the gunsights. He built a small library of books that addressed force in robust, why duck terms.

In *No Second Place Winner,* written by Bill Jordan, a six-and-a-half-foot Texan "lanky as a beef critter eating grease-wood," who could blast a Ping-Pong ball before it dropped to the ground, hit aspirin pills, and split playing cards edgewise ("His .357 must have radar!"), the machismo was resplendent. Holster styles, positions of tilt, tales of the Border Patrol and Texas Rangers, hip draw versus cross draw, pistol grips, and, of course, fast draw were detailed with dry, stony humor. "If he has to use [his gun], he will be playing for keeps . . . ," Jordan philosophizes. "There are no excuses for lack of dexterity . . .

failure to develop efficiency with that tool to the fullest can be attributed only to lack of sincerity, laziness or stupidity." Among the wealth of peppery tips ("before hostilities are opened, never make a threatening motion without carrying it through," "a prudent man will not rely upon hip shooting at distances greater than 7 yards," "your shot will probably go off at navel level if you are thinking strongly of a high chest or throat hit," "you learn by experience—assuming survival"), the credo is spelled out in capital letters: "There is NO SECOND PLACE WINNER IN A GUN FIGHT!!!!!" Jordan considered the .38 Special accurate but not quite powerful enough; the .45 Colt, .44 Special Cartridge, and .44 Magnum too powerful (spoiling a quick second shot); and espoused instead the .357 Magnum, barrel length four inches, with a smooth pistol grip, no checkering. Dallas had a four-inch .357 Magnum with wooden stocks from which he carefully sanded away the checkering. Besides accelerating his combat speed, this also reduced the girth of the grip for what he considered his small hand. He positioned his belt holster just shy of his right rear pocket, FBI style. He purchased speed loaders; in essence, circular clips that police use to reload in a hurry. Jordan nursed the novice gunfighter over any "natural disinclination to pull the trigger at all when your weapon is pointed at a human . . . To aid in overcoming this reluctance it is helpful if you can will yourself to think of your opponent as a mere target and not as a human being." Rex Appelgate had similar advice in another of Dallas's texts, *Kill or Get Killed* (subtitled "Riot Control Techniques, Manhandling and Close Combat for Police and the Military"). "Neither wars nor individual combat can be won by a defensive spirit . . . Once a man has a pistol or revolver in his hand, it should be considered that it is there for immediate use against an enemy. There should not be any hesitation in using it if conditions require its use." Concluded Jordan, "So don't forget: with enough determination you can win even when you appear to be losing—just keep shooting." His adios: "Good hunting."

"Some people have hobbies out there," said one of the trapper's friends. "You know, one man will do beautiful silver work, another man will work leather. Claude's was deadly force." Since his first days in Paradise, a handgun had completed Dallas's outfit. His .22 automatic became a .357 Magnum revolver with wood stocks, wood because "he wouldn't be caught dead using rubber stocks," according to a friend. "Rubber was twentieth century." By the end of the decade, having shot thousands of practice rounds and dropped animals in their tracks farther away than most people could see them, having integrated the advice of master gunslingers, and exercised his marksmanship alongside a police officer, he was frankly *comfortable* in situations.

"I remember one night in McDermitt," said Gary Rose. "There were some pretty high stakes at a card game, and Claude just took off his money belt and laid it on the table. There were drunk Indians and yahoos there who'd knife you for four bits, but hell, no trouble. I don't think I'd lay five dollars on the table. But Claude got by. He always got by." His hair was long, shoulder length. "He let his hair grow," said Cortland Nielsen. "But in this book here, the Bible, it says that long hair is a woman's beauty and it's filth on a man. I told Claude, as long as you're out on the desert, then it's a little bit of protective covering, there's a little reason there. But in here it's filth on a man. I told him so, too." In cowboy country, longhairs got barbered with sheep shears, and in Cheyenne one even got castrated with shears. Dallas had credibility, though. He didn't fight, he didn't bluff, he didn't boast. He didn't need to. He had a presence, a dignity to his posture, even an appeal-

ing aloofness. When other men at his table were headhuddling,
their elbows crowding a conversation between the beer bottles,
Dallas would be erect, removed, never conspicuous, but very
obviously present. "Claude met all the criteria," said another
friend. "He was soft-spoken, self-sufficient and independent,
and he minded his own business." He avoided confrontation.
He didn't like to argue. A story is told that one night in the
Gem Bar he made the mistake of talking to a stranger's girl-
friend. Invited outside to pay the consequences, Dallas touched
his belt and quietly informed the man, "I think you should
know I carry a gun." No more dispute. "I never heard of Claude
hitting a man," said one man. "Never. He had that gun twenty-
four hours a day." It was more than a gun, though. Dallas had
control. Obviously intelligent and capable, the young man impressed people as able. He could have been anything he wanted
to be, people said, a brain surgeon or a bank teller or a salesman. But he had chosen to become a buckaroo and a trapper.
He had willed it and shaped himself and made the dream come
true. It was a simple matter of discipline. Deep in the heart of
whiskey country, he drank fruit juice, forcing himself not to
end like so many Paradise men do, in combat with the Bottle.
One night he drank himself into a fog and discovered next
morning that his favorite hat had been either stolen or lost. The
fact that he couldn't remember, that he had been out of control, disturbed him. There would be no repeats of that care-
lessness because it was his firm conviction that "you're on
your own."

Nowhere was that more evident than when he was gone
wintering, holed up in a cave or lost to the world on the
Owyhee. Out there, his language told you, he was prey to the
harshest season in a harsh territory, "born of the land where
the law was not kindly to the flesh." "Survival out here in the

desert," stated one deputy, "is twice the survival you'll find any-where else. It's that much more austere." "Don't you get lone-some?" a girl once asked him. The trapper didn't deny it nor did he grandstand with the solitude. He just reckoned how "you get used to it." In the Owyhee, between veils of snow squall, on a stage plagued by fog, wind, and isolation, Dallas wrote his own rules of conduct. They were necessarily rigid, for he was "ten miles from hell and a thousand from nowhere." Over and over he demonstrated to himself that his way was *the* way. It worked for him. When he needed meat, he shot it. If someone trespassed on his territory, as happened one year, he simply uprooted the man's traps and threw them in a pile. He trapped according to the season that presented itself physically, as thick, unbroken fur, not by the arbitrary "season" defined in Fish and Game brochures. Even some game wardens would admit that the cat season was a "backdoor" constraint imposed on state Fish and Game departments by federal agencies, which were mainly controlled by antitrappers and environ-mentalists. Game laws irritated other trappers, too. There were so many of them and they made such little sense.

"Pinheaded laws," Santy Mendietta cursed them. "Hen-house rules and regulations. It don't matter if it's the preacher's son or the game warden himself. If he's trapping these days he's going to break one of them." Besides obtaining a state-issued license, the trapper had to observe a host of rules concerning the structure and placement of his traps. Traps had to be placed two hundred feet from county roads. Their bait could not be exposed, or if exposed had to be placed at least twenty feet from the nearest trap (because other predators such as endangered or out-of-season animals would be attracted to the meat or fluttering bird wings). The trapper's identification number had to be stamped on each set. Every trap had to be "gapped" or "eagle protected," which meant welding a pair of beads onto each jaw. When closed, a ⅜-inch gap in the jaws would theoretically allow raptors to survive with their thin legs intact. ("Silly," Mendietta contended. "An eagle caught in a trap is a dead eagle, regardless of whether you turn him loose or not. An eagle hunts with his feet. If he's got a broken toe, and he will if he's trapped, then he can't hunt. And he'll starve to death.") A ninety-six-hour visitation law required the trapper to visit his traps at least once every four days (to put the animals out of their misery). In addition, there were varying periods of time for various districts during which various furbearers could be caught legally. There was no season for coyotes, but the bobcat season was short, only twenty or thirty days. Take a cat before or after the specified dates and the trapper faced a hefty fine and confiscation of the pelt. Too strict, trappers complained. Too inflexible. "Say a man's got five hundred coyote traps out and the cat season's over. And he has a cat, accidentally caught," Mendietta conjectured. "Hell, how are you going to let a cat go?" Trappers ridiculed the trapping rules that coincided with the ascendancy of environmentalism in federal grazing regulations. Like the cowboys, they saw themselves besieged by sissies seeking to steal their income and bleed dry an American heritage. "I can't tell you why these laws ever came in," said Mendietta. "These laws, most of them, come about in the last ten years. And trappers been trapping in the country for some one hundred fifty."

Dallas ignored the rules. He had a trapping license, but there was no way around that really. An accidental cat hide or two out of season could be discussed with the game warden, but only after you had shown a modicum of respect . . . a license. Beyond that, he felt he knew better. "He had a funny sort of philosophy about trapping animals," said Hoyt Wilson.

"He'd go into an area and survey it, check the cat sign and the coyote sign, decide how many animals he was going to take, and take them. And then he'd move on. He said, 'I'm a better conservationist than the Fish and Game, I don't know why they bother me.'" Not surprisingly, they did bother him.

His first encounter with a game warden was in 1976. A Nevada Fish and Game officer named Dale Elliot had found his illegally baited trapline near the Cortez Mountains in central Nevada, and picked up some of the sets. The two met in Dallas's winter camp, a citation was written up, and the trapper posted a hundred-dollar cash bond. A date was set for him to appear in Eureka before the justice of the peace, at which time he forfeited the money and was given back his traps. A year later Elliot paid a second visit, this time with another game warden, to a camp on Savory Creek sixty miles farther south. After checking his license, the wardens had a cup of tea with Dallas. Before leaving, they obliged him by towing his pickup to start it.

The following winter he moved his trapping operation out of Elliot's district to more familiar ground, the Bloody Run Hills that loom behind Paradise Hill. There, too, Fish and Game located him . . . or tried to . . . and confiscated guns and traps. The peculiar circumstances of the encounter underscored the cat-and-mouse game some hunters and trappers play with game wardens and vice versa. A young and affable Nevada game warden named Gene Weller was making a routine check of traplines late one afternoon, when he came across a number of illegally baited sets. Because of the location of the traps and the late hour, Weller decided against waiting for the owner of the traps. Instead, he confiscated three or four of them, leaving his business card and a note stating why the traps had been seized and whom to contact. Early next morning, as

Weller was returning to the canyon, he saw a red Jeep moving toward the canyon mouth. He parked his truck in an arroyo and waited until the driver had departed on foot up the canyon, then drove closer, and prepared for that rare event in a game warden's career—the arrest of a violator caught red-handed.

"I waited all day," Weller said. "I waited and waited. It was in the winter and the canyon was slipperier than all get-out, and I thought finally, this guy has slipped and broken his leg. By then it was dark. I called for a sheriff's backup and got a couple of deputies.

"The three of us went up. One of the deputies checked the Jeep and found a rifle. He told me it was loaded, with an unexpended [and therefore illegal] round in the chamber. I pulled the coil wire off the Jeep, just in case, and took it with me. We went up the canyon.

"Well, I tracked him in the frozen snow, tracked him to the first trap site, and my business card which I'd hung on a bait wire was gone. At this point I circled around with a flashlight. There was another set of tracks coming down, but not on the trail. So I tracked these. Finally the tracks went up a side hill and I lost the track. I later found that he was in fact sitting on the mountain watching me watch for him. He was probably chuckling the whole time. In retrospect, he could have blown me away at any time that day."

The three officers retreated to their vehicles, confiscated the rifle and a revolver from the Jeep, and left. A few days later Dallas appeared at the county courthouse. He denied that the traps had been his or that the rifle had been loaded, and he wanted the guns back. Weller had no evidence connecting Dallas with the traps, and when the deputy who had opened the rifle was questioned about it, he declined to swear under oath that the round had been a live one. Weller could do nothing but sign the guns over to Dallas. The trapper had bluffed and won. For a while longer, he stayed and talked with Weller, expounding on his philosophy that there should be a subsistence law allowing a man to eat game when he needed it, and at one point, Weller remembered, "[Claude] told me, 'You are welcome in my camp.' His camp was very important to him, I found out later. 'But,' he said, 'leave your badge outside.' And I told him, 'Claude, I can't leave my badge outside.' And he said, 'Well, don't come into my camp then.'" After that, Weller felt the man should be taken "special care of," approached with caution.

Weller figured again in Dallas's affairs, again indirectly. Returning to Winnemucca with one of several arrested poachers one night, the game warden ran low on gas near Paradise Hill and stopped at George Nielsen's bar, which boasted two pumps. The pumps were locked up, but with a flourish and as a favor he expected to be remembered, Nielsen found the key and loaned Weller some gas. Sometime later, Dallas found two cougars caught in his trapline on the same day, an unheard-of circumstance. It is illegal to trap mountain lions; they can be hunted only with rifles. By law, Dallas should have contacted the authorities to drug and remove the big cats. Instead, he collected on his good fortune and dispatched the animals. The hides ended up back at Paradise Hill, the object of much envy and comment. In a telling display of vicarious pride, George Nielsen insisted on draping the large, tawny pelts over his pool table for all to admire. A deputy and a highway patrolman on their way to Winnemucca happened to stop in for a beer, saw the pelts, and mentioned them later to Gene Weller. Weller wasted no time in obtaining a search warrant, driving to Paradise Hill and slapping Nielsen with a citation. He also confiscated the cougar pelts. The bar owner was astounded. Figuring that his gasoline favor had earned him an informal and lasting immunity from Fish and Game, the citation and subsequent court case (which Nielsen's lawyer finally got dismissed) embittered him. Thereafter he freely blustered that Weller should be shot. Coming from Nielsen, it was not an overly relevant remark. His list of men who should be killed was reportedly as long as it was strident. Just talk.

In 1978 Dallas talked his brother Stuart and a buckaroo friend named Steve Nelson into a grand adventure. Since early childhood Claude had been dreaming of Alaska. At long last he had the money, time, and wilderness skills to go north and harvest the boyhood legends. By canoe, the little band of men crossed the gigantic Great Slave Lake in the Northwest Territories of Canada and descended the Mackenzie River over a thousand miles toward the Arctic Circle and tundra. Fearful of grizzly bears, they spent some nights on sandbars in the middle of the river. For three months they canoed, fishing and hunting for their food. At one point Claude Dallas bagged a huge bighorn sheep. No game wardens regulated their passage. It was hundreds of idyllic miles between one river town and the next. The trip ended in Dawson, near the Yukon-Alaska border, with the men broke but happy. George Nielsen wired money to them in Whitehorse, and Dallas returned, a minor hero among friends, with stories and snapshots of the great voyage.

In January 1979, Dallas moved his trapline to Star Valley on the Owyhee Desert, taking over a line cabin in territory that had two owners, Tom Pedroli of McDermitt, the owner in title, and Don Carlin and his two sons, the owner by trapper's law. The Carlin family leased the 45 Ranch down the South Fork of the Owyhee River, and supplemented their income with cat and coyote furs caught in the winter. Though Pedroli had given his permission to Dallas for use of the line cabin, the Carlins had clearly regarded the trapper's sudden arrival as a violation of their trapping area. Their first confrontation occurred as the interloper was cleaning up the cabin. Carlin showed up in a pickup and his two sons rode in on horseback. The trapper was asked what he was doing. Dallas mocked them. "I talked to Don about maybe I'd hang some meat up," he said. "Maybe I asked him if he'd seen much Fish and Game. I invited them into camp and I invited them into the cabin. And I remember I had a jug on the table and they had a few drinks." The Carlins wanted him out. "They made it pretty clear they did not approve much of my presence there." Dallas was imperturbable. Immovable. "I told them my camp was always open. I told them if they were in the area to stop and warm up, and cook up, and there is a spare bed there." He didn't budge.

For a month he ran his trapline, a half dozen sets in Idaho, seventy-five sets south of the Nevada border. The season on cats was two or three weeks longer in Nevada than in Idaho that year, but the possibility of an Idaho game warden troubling him for pelts taken south of the state border and dried north of it didn't faze Dallas. He observed his own rules. When he decided to wrap it up in February, he hauled out the bulk of his gear in a truck, then returned for the rest and to give the cabin a final cleaning. By the time he got back to the cabin a day or two later, there was a business card stuck in the cabin's screen door.

"It was a standard printed card of Idaho Fish and Game," Dallas recalled. "I can't remember what else it had on it but the name of the officer . . . Bill Pogue. William H. Pogue or whatever. On the back of the card there was a note. 'I'll check on you later.'" The card, and especially the note, rankled Dallas. "I thought it was a hell of a way to introduce yourself. I was a legal tenant and it was private property. Just the card had been left. It could have been something a little more civil. I thought it was . . . inappropriate."

Spring came on. Dallas ran the South Fork of the Owyhee in a canoe all the way to Rome, Oregon, and then made some money doing "custom" farm work for a Paradise Valley rancher. He was restless, though. The cow outfits had gone to hell, game wardens bothered him, and the BLM was everywhere. Things had gotten close in Paradise, and there were other adventures to engage. Alaska had infected him with its splendid openness and freedom. After Alaska, he told friends, he fancied going to sea in his own boat . . . the province of Jack London . . . and maybe to Australia. He spent the summer in California cutting timber. By September his mind was made up to leave for Alaska. He made some more money "ripping ground" for a potato farmer on the west side of Sand Pass Road, and was preparing to pack up for Alaska when George Nielsen reminded him of a promise.

A furrier in Seattle had told Nielsen that with twenty or thirty bobcat pelts and fifteen hundred dollars for the cutting and sewing, Liz Nielsen could have a thirty-thousand-dollar coat. Dallas had earlier promised to catch the cats, possibly to pay off a debt to the bar owner, and now Nielsen pressed him for the pelts. The trapper thought about it. There was no urgent appointment to keep in Alaska, and this would complete his obligations in Paradise. One last winter wouldn't be so bad, and he agreed to stay. He even had in mind the place to winter out of. On the first night of his spring canoe trip, he had stopped deep in a beautiful gorge at a place called Bull Camp. On December 3, a caravan of friends and vehicles transported him eighty miles out along the pipeline road, then west to a cattle trough and drift fence on the 45 Ranch's BLM lease, landmarks to the Bull Camp trailhead. Down he went, through curtains of thick, wet snow. "I wasn't in there that winter for money," he said. "Money had little to do with my being in Bull Camp. I was after cats. Coyotes had already started to rub. It was very warm." Thirty pelts and he would be free of the stale dream Paradise had become.

Back in Paradise Hill, George Nielsen bragged about the trapper, telling one and all how tough he was. "The statement was made there in that bar," said a patron, "that no one was going to move in on Claude at the South Fork of the Owyhee because Claude would kill them. You don't draw against Claude because Claude will kill you." Everyone figured it was just more raw bluster.

# Chapter 5

*T*HERE was a parable in Paradise, one of those little mirrors people hold up to see themselves. Les Stewart of the 96 Ranch, the valley's most august rancher and something of a patriarch, told the story best. It was about rude law and perpetual innocence.

"This old Indian," he related, "Albert Skedaddle we called him, he worked here for years. And the Indians, they like to take the offal from the beef. They take the head and get the tongue and the brains, and there's a lot of good meat on the head they use. And then they like to have all the other offal, the intestines and the stomach. Practically everything inside of the cow they have some use for. So every time we butchered, he would get a big old barley sack and get in his old car and then go to McDermitt with it. He wouldn't go around the high-way, 'cause time didn't mean much to him. He'd go over the mountain.

"And he was going along over there one day, he said, and the game warden stopped him. The game warden saw he had something in the sack, and he was suspicious, I guess, that he had a bunch of fish or sage hens or something. So the game warden, kind of rude, he didn't ask him or anything, he just took the old boy's sack away from him and dumped it out into the middle of the road. And all these guts and hearts and lungs and the whole thing fell out on the road. And Albert said the game warden was so badly surprised that he just stood there and looked at him for a while and turned around without a word and got in his car and left. He left Albert standing there with all this stuff laying in the gravel."

There, succinctly, was the way it was. In the middle of nowhere, the man with the badge finds you, harries and bends you, dumps your hard-earned meal on the road, and then drives away. It explained, in part, why the 130 Idahoans who came searching for the body of Bill Pogue in mid-February 1981 were viewed as an unwelcome swarm. Headed by Tim Nettleton, their horses were corraled at an old BLM station north of George Nielsen's bar, and the small army camped at the rodeo fairgrounds in Winnemucca. Radio gear, first-aid equipment, tents, and food were provided by the Idaho BLM. Water, portable toilets, and maps came from the Nevada BLM. Of the hundred-plus volunteers, a handful were from Nevada, none from Paradise. Even the Humboldt County sher-iff's department declined to participate, citing tight manpower. (Privately, Sheriff Weston was furious at this latest encroach-ment on his jurisdiction. "You don't bring down people from another state the way they did," he said, "their air search team and Jeep patrols and all that other bullshit, that's unethical. We had our people." Privately as well, many Idaho authorities felt Weston's "people" were scandalously relaxed about finding Claude Dallas.) The searchers drove pickups with Idaho license plates and bumper stickers that read "Fightin' Crime Owyhee County Style." But this was emphatically not Owyhee County.

Besides that parable about Albert Skedaddle, and no one clearly associated it with the Bull Camp violence, there was another, more tangible reason for Paradise's detachment. As it turned out, people had known Bill Pogue. Now, with his body hidden somewhere in their midst, stories about the man began to haunt Paradise, where he had been a game warden twenty years earlier, and the ION region at large. The most damning and fabulous of all the tales is told by the Reverend Laverne Inzer, a flamboyant crackerjack of a Southern Baptist who had adopted Paradise Valley as part of his arid parish.

"It was about 1960–62," he recalls. "I was out fishing with another man of the cloth. And Pogue comes up on us and he says, 'Had any luck?' I say, 'Oh yeah.' Then he snaps, 'Well, let me see your fishing license.' 'Well'"—and the reverend has told the tale so often his inflections are theatrical—"'all right,' I said, 'it's here in my billfold.'"

The reverend raises his voice with Old Testament wrath, imitating the game warden. "'Well. Let me see 'em.'"

And his voice becomes reasonable again, his own voice. "'Okay, you're welcome to it.' Pogue looks at it and throws it on the ground. I pick it up. 'Who's your partner?' he asks. 'A Catholic priest,' I say. 'I'd like to catch that so-and-so.' I say, 'Oh? Well, you don't want to do that.' 'Oh? You going to tell me how to run my business?' 'Hey, fella,' I say, 'me and him, we're proper, we don't do that.' So we sit there and had an exchange over it.

"Suddenly the Catholic priest stood up and started running as fast as he could run. 'What's that so-and-so running for?' I say, 'I don't know.' Pogue says, 'Halt! Stop in the name of the law, I said halt!'" Inzer laughs. "The priest just kept on running. Pogue pulled his old hogleg out and wham, puts a shot in the air. 'Next shot'll be between your blankety-blank eyes.' That priest just raised up his eyes and took off again." Inzer laughs again.

"I stepped toward Pogue. I was going to hit him or something, but I was going to stop him from shooting that boy. And boy, he turned that hogleg on me and it looked as big as a drinking glass. 'Another step,' he says, 'and I'll blow your damned head off.'" Inzer pauses for effect.

"And what happened, that priest had been chasing a baby porcupine. Then I made a remark I wish I hadn't made. I said, 'Pogue, you're going to pull that gun on somebody one of these days who got a gun, and you're not going to live to tell about it.'" The reverend's twenty-year-old prophecy gave muscle to the multiplying tales of harassment and elevated Pogue to the rank of scapegoat, and the fact of his death to the rank of destiny. He became darkness and thunder in the valleys of wildflowers and light. As Sheriff Nettleton put it, "After he was shot, Bill Pogue paid the price for every game warden that's ever tromped on somebody out in the wilderness." He took on all the worst elements of all the worst game wardens anyone had ever heard of. He became the enemy.

"There are stories common to types of people," said Jerry Thiessen, a wildlife biologist and Bill Pogue's best friend. "The Fish and Game people have one that goes, you know, 'A Californian tried to bring a dead mule through the game check station yesterday.' If I've heard that once, I've heard it a thousand times. If you ask, did you see it?, they say, 'No. But somebody told me about it.' Every year the same story . . . it's always 'yesterday,' 'California license plates,' and 'the thing still had horseshoes on.'

"One that's told about Fish and Game is 'We saw you up in a helicopter throwing firecrackers to scare the game away.' We've never done it in our life. But they'll say, 'My grandfather even got the number off the helicopter.' Another common one is 'He'd arrest his grandmother.' Another one you hear is, the game warden stands up from a camper's fish dinner and the camper tells him, 'You could have arrested me for that, but now you've eaten the evidence.'"

In fact, people in Paradise swore Pogue would enter their camp at dinner, eat their fowl or venison, then check their licenses. He would borrow their horses in the morning to check fishermen on the mountain, and in the afternoon check the man he had borrowed the horse from. It was said he entered a family's home while the rancher was out herding cattle, and forced the housewife to empty her freezer for a meat check. When the rancher returned, went the tale, he properly grabbed a rifle and drove Pogue off. Another time, Pogue stopped a sick old man and forced him to empty his truck of firewood in the middle of the road on the chance it might be covering fresh game. It wasn't, and without a word or a hand reloading, he just drove off . . . shades of Albert Skedaddle. And though no one ever thought to complain to the Nevada or Idaho departments while he was still alive, they complained after he was dead. Two men had been gunned down at Bull Camp, but only one death seemed to matter. Once the gunsmoke cleared, Conley Elms became trivial, a 280-pound bear of a man who had happened into the wrong place and time and died too young to have a past. Pogue, though . . . as the saga developed . . . it was he who had cornered Dallas down in the pit of that Owyhee gorge, a Goliath hampering the lone wolf's freedom. Even mute and still somewhere on their desert floor, Pogue could not rest in peace. Few had actually known the man . . . twenty years had passed . . . but no one, it seemed, had not met his image.

Early on Bill Pogue had been fascinated with the world of animals, one of those children forever gone in the foothills, poking beneath rocks and investigating streams, studying secret motions. Even before starting elementary school in rural Bakersfield, California, he was banding birds, learning their songs and names. He taught himself to draw birds and other animals, learned to fish (and yet never really took to guns and hunting the way his younger brother, Eddie, did). Except for brief periods, he never departed from the garden of animals the rest of his life, stuck in boyish awe of the cleaner motions.

During the Korean War he held a ridge through one winter, taking shrapnel and suffering frostbite on his toes and the bottoms of his feet. But he refused to talk about those times. While still in the Marines, he met his wife, Dee. They started a family. Dee worked while he attended Humboldt State University, studying wildlife management. During the third summer of school, he left his wife and infant son, Steve, for three months in the Brooks Range of Alaska to tag salmon for a remote stream survey. "And it was," emphasized his best friend, Jerry Thiessen, "remote." He thrived on the remoteness.

After graduation, he took a job with Nevada Fish and Game and moved his family to Las Vegas, Nevada, to begin a long spiral of assignments and migrations that would end at Bull Camp. His childhood fascination with wildlife was now a professional and educated one, informed by field studies and department policy and backed by the law. From the beginning he was a game warden, underpaid, overworked. "Some people enter Fish and Game enforcement as an entree into wildlife research," observed Thiessen, a researcher with Idaho Fish and Game. "But it doesn't take them long to begin feeling that what they're doing is worthwhile. Once a man's been in law enforcement for four or five years, there's a very high probability he'll always be in enforcement." Pogue was.

With his transfer in 1959 to Winnemucca, Pogue moved square into northern Nevada cow country, and got his first good taste of the Owyhee region. The Owyhee was his kind of territory. "No roads and no houses and you stand out there," his son, Steve, said, "and all you hear is the birds and the wind." He got to know the people of Paradise Valley and the surrounding communities, borrowed their horses, ate their beefsteak, venison, and fish with them . . . and checked them for game violations. And if they had broken a law, he cited them. He never forgot the Owyhee.

Against his better judgment, Pogue was talked into becoming the chief of police in Winnemucca in 1963. The department had a reputation for brutality and corruption, and it was felt that here was the right man to clean things up. Knowing how distasteful the job would be, even before accepting it Pogue clearly limited his term to one year. True to his word, in 1965 he took a job with Idaho Fish and Game, and soon had his family situated in a piece of Eden called Garden Valley, an hour's drive north of Boise. In sharp contrast to Humboldt County, Garden Valley was a lush, green region with trees, rivers, and creeks. The crops were fat and green, not brown, and the desert was far away. For the next eight years the Pogues inhabited a department house, a cabin really, with a wood stove, redwood paint, a hot tin roof, and a makeshift stone chimney. For eight years they perched on the side of a hill surrounded by huge evergreens draped with moss and, in the spring, crowded with wildflowers. They slept with the sound of the river. These were happy times for Pogue.

For the longest time he could not bring himself to believe that any animal could be as wanton and destructive as man. And so against all the breathers of superstitions and backwoods folklore and the men who ought to have known, he championed the cougar. It is an elegant creature, upward of seven feet long and two hundred pounds, with a dark mystique spun partly from its stealth and solitariness, partly from its killing talents and ability to disappear into the land. Ever ready to rebut its detractors, Pogue would quote facts from an extensive cougar study Idaho Fish and Game had conducted in the early 1960s, in which the cougar was portrayed as a misunderstood yet vital check and balance in the cycle of elk and deer populations, a savior with claws and fist-sized paws. According to Sterling Alley, a legendary Idaho rancher and friend of the game warden's, for Pogue "the cougar was a saint." Even after Alley had shown him the carcasses to prove that the cat was not just a carnivore but a killer that would track a herd and pull down five and six deer and take no more than a bite from each, Pogue defended the cougar with unusual doggedness. Possibly it was the cougar's instinct for solitude that Bill Pogue appreciated so much, for he had it himself. Beyond that was his faith in the basic decency of animals.

He was a mountain man at heart, bonded to remote geography and the animals with a gruff, four-wheel-drive sort of pantheism. He would stop his pickup just to watch a sunset or listen to thunder or look at the trees. "He saw a lot of beauty." His philosophy was that no one owned the land, a feeling that led him to explore literature about Indians and their broken treaties with the U.S. government. "He felt that it was a sin when streams were degraded," said Thiessen. "He hated the waste of nature." Pogue was well aware that the mountain men had looted the rivers and marshes of beaver, not culling or harvesting them or attempting, however crudely, to maintain their source of wealth. They had taken. They had been wanton. He understood also the role of power and politics in the nineteenth- and twentieth-century American wilderness. And while he lamented with Frémont, the great pathfinder, that "that race of trappers who formerly lived in [the] recesses, had almost entirely disappeared," he could see that for all their buckskin mythos, they had been the earliest tentacle of a destructive beast, and that it was up to him to check it. "If there is a future for wild things," he wrote on a photo of Thiessen and him camping in some Owyhee canyon, "then it is the burden of those who have reached further than me to save them for the rest of us. It will be done by those whose convictions were forged in campfire. Bill."

The clash between civilization and wilderness, modern man and mountain man, late twentieth- and early nineteenth-century values, touched Pogue deeply, though he never said much about it. For him the clash was not an apocalyptic one. It was simply the turning of the wheel. This inevitable process spared only a few relics and left a nostalgic ache. He had read Vardis Fisher's elegiac *Mountain Man* (which Robert Redford made into *Jeremiah Johnson*). He also never forgot how his friend Sterling Alley once climbed a tree in pursuit of a bobcat with nothing more than a pigging string (a leather thong for tying calves' legs during branding), and how he fought and subdued the cat and brought it to earth where, scratched and bleeding, he released it . . . all "just to see if I could do it." Pogue saw the spirit of bygone times all around him. Like Dallas, he wouldn't have minded if the stories about Alley or the buckskinned meat eaters in *Mountain Man* had been true about himself. To an extent, they were. Horses had gone over on him. He'd almost died from rattlesnake bites, and again had almost died after chewing barley stalks treated with poison for ground squirrels. He had lost the sight in his right eye in a camping accident. Another time he had barely survived a truck accident that occurred sixty miles from the nearest help. But these seemed just tame accidents to him, pedestrian next to the spirit of men like Alley. Pogue was content with the man he was, and yet he couldn't help but see the man he might have been. "My brother was born a hundred years too late," said Eddie Pogue.

He spent time in bunkhouses and at line camps; he knew old buckaroos and cowboy songs, and loved to pack a horse up into the primitive areas to check the high mountain lakes and live on the bare necessities and be alone. His favorite area never ceased to be the Owyhee Desert. "He loved the remoteness," reiterated Thiessen, "the vastness. Every chance he got, he would assist another officer in Owyhee County." Pogue and Thiessen spent weeklong vacations in the desert, and with his brother Eddie he explored on horseback, even going to the plateau above Bull Camp. Once, said Eddie Pogue, they found an ancient Shoshone camp. "Bill showed me a beautiful arrowhead and told me all about the site by looking at stone chips. But he wouldn't let me pick anything up. He said, 'Just leave it like it is.'" That was his ethic. He took very seriously his role as custodian of the land, guardian of the past.

On first meeting the game warden, no one suspected him of sensitivity, much less poetry. He was so awkward and hard and imposing, many insisted so arrogant, a man with that cold, dead eye and bad humor and galling, go-to-hell manner. He was to many people just a badge. His artwork exposed a softer man, though, an artist with whom he never quite reconciled himself. His drawings embarrassed him, even in front of his family, and most ended up in a wad in the garbage can. He had never taken a lesson in his life, drawing was just something he had always done. As a boy, he had gotten fired from a Bakersfield grocery store for sketching on cereal boxes, and he delighted friends by drawing their portraits on beer mugs. The quality of his work was just as surprising to people as the fact of it. It was painstaking and laborious and sentimental. His drawings were done with a Rapidograph in total privacy, no one around, and because he had just one good eye and because he did not use line hatching but stippled with ink dots, Pogue needed a magnifying glass to draw. He could work only in fifteen-minute bursts. Then he would rest his eye for fifteen minutes and return to the piece. Laboring in this fashion, he was good for two hours before having to quit for the night, and some of his works could take eighty nights to be finished.

In the last years of his life, Pogue approached a Boise art gallery about displaying some of his pieces. He was shy ("Inside," said Thiessen, "he felt it would have been a sign of weakness to publicly show his appreciation for things"), and more comfortable giving his drawings away than selling them. People liked his work. Like "Charlie" Russell, the cowboy-artist so dear to westerners, his work addressed the smaller moments in hard and hearty lives. In "Lady Friends Comin'," an elderly cowhand barbers the one hair on his buddy's bald head. "First Grade Reader" shows an old, leathery buckaroo taking time out with a mug of coffee and a first-grade primer. The most popular of his drawings, "Cowboy and Bird," presents a grizzled, squinting Basco feeding a bug to a nestling on his fingertips. In "The Trapper," a fierce-looking trapper stares at the viewer as if he were trespassing, a dead wolf at his feet. He drew Indians, animals, cowboys, and mountain men—those things that moved upon the land. But he never drew the land itself. Perhaps it was too big or too eloquent all by itself.

Retirement was out of the question. His work consumed him. "He'd tell my mom on Sunday, I've got the day off and I'm not going to do anything but sit here and watch television and drink ice tea," recalled Steve Pogue. "But around one in the afternoon he'd jump up and put on his shirt and shoes and jump in the pickup and say, 'Well, I'm just going to work for a couple of hours.' He'd be gone until ten at night in the middle of the winter to keep people from the deer and elk." Pogue consistently put in more hours than any other warden in Idaho. To each game warden the department allocated gas money. When his monthly stipend was exhausted, Pogue would fill the gas tank of the department truck from his own pocket. He had a mission, keenly felt. The wilderness was being ravaged, the animals extinguished.

In the arena of modern environmentalism, there are a pronounced right wing and left wing, both of which scrap and scramble for public attention, funds, and power. Both clamor for the title "environmentalist." On one side are those purists who would preserve the wilderness in a bell jar, even to the exclusion of ecophile hikers. At the opposite extreme are people who insist that the environment must pay its own rent in the form of being grazed, mined, or drilled. Bill Pogue stood in between. He thought in broad terms . . . species, herds, the ecosystem, the public, the law. A walking, eating, breeding, renewable resource—the wildlife—had to be managed. Well before it was the fashion to look at the quality of herds, not just their population numbers, Pogue was keeping herd composition records. He was counting them, noting their condition, their migration paths, calving grounds, and grazing ranges. He tended the sick, shot the mortally wounded, and watched them starve to death in the winter. One local herd's migration path was intersected by a reservoir, and year after year he had to stand by while deer drowned attempting to cross thin ice. The biologists' classic answer was that if the feed was too scarce, more animals should be shot. One director had gone so far as to decree, in effect, "Let the bastards starve." Pogue argued that, to the contrary, it was all right to throw out a few bales of hay if it meant bringing a few animals through the winter. He boned up on facts and data, trapped deer with Sterling Alley and marked them, and bridged the interdepartmental gap between game wardens and biologists. He referred to an already high mortality rate from poachers and predators, and slyly pointed out that the community was waiting to see just how humanely Fish and Game solved the problem. Beneath the professionalism was pathos. "He asked me, you ever see a herd of nine hundred deer starve to death?" said his brother. "Enough to make you throw up. Bill would talk about that with tears in his eyes. It was like something personal was being taken from him. Those animals belonged to him."

Department policy was just beginning to undergo a philosophical evolution, and Pogue found support for his idea in Jerry Thiessen, one of the more enlightened biologists. "In the mid-sixties and seventies the emphasis shifted from how much to harvest, how many to kill, to what kinds of herds do we have left. Bill's position during that time was more right than wrong. His position on what kinds of things we should be doing was much closer to what we're doing now than what we were doing then." The deer got their hay. The hunting season was reduced from three months to its present three weeks.

In 1973 Pogue was promoted to district manager and transferred to the Boise office. It was a desk job and he loathed it, declaring it a demotion. Paperwork sat in front of him while he gazed through the window at the distant Owyhee Mountains. The move had certain advantages, though, chief among them that the Owyhee County district was now under his control, and he could help patrol it. Of particular interest to him was a herd of California bighorn sheep recently introduced to the desert from British Columbia. He spent time with the herd, photographing the sheep. Whenever a Fish and Game plane flew overhead to do a winter head count, he was sure to ask how they were doing. He did what he could to protect them from the ubiquitous poachers. Among big-game trophy hunters, there is a coveted collection of heads called the "Grand Slam." The collection consists of a head and shoulders from each of the four wild sheep native to North America. Permits for a single sheep can sell for as much as sixty-six thousand dollars; illegal hunts can be arranged for thirty to fifty thousand dollars. Some men have completed four or five Grand Slams at a cost of a million dollars or more. Hunting them legally is for most a once-in-a-lifetime privilege. Hunters submit their names to a lottery from which a handful of tags is awarded each year. Because they are so difficult to hunt, the bighorns on the Owyhee and surrounding range can fetch up to ten thousand dollars or more per head. When Pogue learned one year that an Arab sheik was planning an illegal big-game hunt in the Owyhee to bag a desert bighorn, he drove to the desert, camouflaged his truck, and, though the sheik never appeared, lived near the herd for the next eleven days.

Poaching and illicit trade in wildlife parts nets $100 million a year in this country. Newly grown elk antlers can fetch up to $120 a pound. Arabs will pay $80,000 for a baby gyrfalcon, coveted for its hunting prowess. Black bears are killed and gutted for their gallbladder (an ingredient in Oriental folk medicine) and claws. Common desert animals like the coyote and rattlesnake all have a price on the market. In pursuit of animals, some poachers use two-way radios, helicopters, fixed-wing aircraft, nightscopes, spotlights, explosives packed with sodium cyanide, and in one recent instance a tank trajectory table to stabilize shots over a half-mile distant.

"Bill had a feeling that there was far more wildlife being extracted by poachers than the records would indicate," said Thiessen. "He felt it was important to get a handle on those poachers. He encountered them frequently, but it's not something he brooded about. It was a matter of fact." In Pogue's world they could wear many masks . . . salmon snaggers, farmers, cougar hunters, ranchers, trappers, physicians, and lawyers . . . and the only way to catch a poacher was to catch him redhanded. Hide-and-seek was the game, with few people ranking a Fish and Game citation even as high as a speeding ticket. Some game wardens will wink at the lesser offenders, for example, the ranchers who bag a stray buck or the fisherman with an extra trout . . . the type of wardens who actually make it a pleasure to be cited. Bill Pogue had a different sort of reputation. He was the Iceman.

"He didn't care who it was," said his son. "He'd have wrote anybody a ticket. He'd write up a ticket on his daughters, his mother or me or you." In fact, after catching his son shooting doves on a power line, he had almost thrown the boy in jail, but finally allowed another warden merely to cite him. Everyone agreed. Pogue would cite his own mother.

"He came into my camp one time ahorseback," recalled Sterling Alley of his own outfitting days, "and when he came in, suddenly I was a total stranger to him. He checked my hunter's license, checked my clients' game, checked the meat on the poles. And left. The next time I seen him, I chewed his ass for being so unfriendly, and he said, 'I was there on business.'" That was Pogue. Business was business. If you didn't like the laws, change them. "Pogue didn't have much finesse, I guess that's the word," said Alley. He was gruff. He could be abrasive. And after he vanished into the desert night, locked in ghostly combat with his killer, people began reminding each other of the reverend's story.

The people closest to Pogue told their own stories. "There was a family with twelve kids in Garden Valley, a log cutter's family, and they had a hell of a time making it in the winter," Steve Pogue recalled. "We never had any deer meat in our freezer, my mom didn't like it. So when he got his tags every year, once in a while my dad would shoot a deer. But every deer he shot went to that poor family or somebody else that needed it." Others remembered him as a gentle man who laughed the day he found a baby's footprints tracking across his freshly varnished table, the sort of man who was sure to be first up in the morning to start a fire and make others a cup of hot coffee, or who would pick flowers for a friend's wife simply because he wanted to.

One night Pogue was in the Owyhee with Nettleton, who sometimes patrolled with him or helped at the roadblock game checks, and they apprehended a man with an illegal deer. After discussion, said Nettleton, "we found out that he wasn't doing it to poach. He was doing it to eat. And the only thing Bill said was, 'If I ever hear in a bar that I turned you loose, you're in trouble.' And let him go." Pogue was, friends and family insist, more flexible than people wanted to believe after Bull Camp. He could be flexible, but he could also be hard—severe— especially, said his brother Eddie, "on the bastard who doesn't give a damn, the hard-core poacher who's got a camp with venison hanging and the traps baited and the hides stretched."

It was like something personal was being taken from him. "He took it real personal." Eddie Pogue was proud. "My brother was a hard-nosed, straight-down-the-line cop. If you had a ticket coming, you got it, especially if you flunked the attitude test. If you were an asshole, then you were going to go to jail or get the ticket."

No one denied that Pogue was territorial and had a manner that could freeze small ponds. And his temper has never been forgotten at the Longhorn Saloon in Garden Valley where they still call it "pogueing 'em" when a pitch player is dealt a poor hand, blows up, and throws his cards into the air. But the people who knew him refused to accept that he drew his gun at Bull Camp, or if he did, as Sterling Alley believes, "only after there was a bullet in him."

He had no particular love for guns and only a passable competence with them, which is ironic not only because daily through half his life he carried the weight of a Smith and Wesson on his hip, but also because he was instrumental in obtaining peace-officer status for the game wardens of Idaho. This empowered them to enforce felony charges outside the misdemeanor realm of game laws, and that in turn justified escalating the game wardens' firearms training. Before he went to Idaho, more than half the officers didn't even carry guns. As the number of assaults on game wardens grew, he organized a group of Fish and Game officers and pressed for more protection.

After Bull Camp, people questioned the need for game wardens to carry guns at all. It was reasoned that London bobbies don't, and get along just fine. Statistics speak of a mounting violence in the wilderness, though, particularly against game wardens. One ten-year study conducted by the Wyoming Fish and Game Department showed that a game warden has roughly seven times the chance of getting shot at or threatened with a gun as a regular peace officer, and almost nine times as great a chance of dying if assaulted. "We go out and find even fishermen carrying guns and big knives," said Michael Elms, Conley's older brother. "It's sort of a Wild West syndrome. We have an air force base down the road here. As soon as they hit the base, some of the men go out and buy a gun, a big knife, and a couple of bandoliers and head out into the hills."

The camps are nearly always armed, and frequently the hunters and fishermen are drunk at night, when game wardens might check through. The machismo can run high under those conditions, and the frontier is that much less illusory once the stars come out and the coyotes howl. Every game warden has stories of the hostility they sometimes encounter. It can be subtle: a frown, a grumble, a loaded rifle accidentally swung in their direction. Or it can be outright, as when two game wardens in Owyhee County ended up in a hospital for trying to check a group's sage-hen take. "People get mad," said Steve Pogue. "There was a family of salmon snaggers up in Bear Valley and they said to my dad, I'm going to throw you in the crick. But my dad never drew his gun on them. And he never got thrown in the crick." Most law officers will tell you there is only one way to react in such situations. "If a fellow's going to hit you," said Nettleton, "by God, you stand your ground. Because if you don't, you're going to get hit."

Caution became second nature to Bill Pogue. It showed in small ways, in restaurants, for instance, where he wouldn't sit with his back to a window or the door. Sterling Alley remembers that just before walking into a camp of cougar hunters, "Pogue reached under his Marlboro coat—one of those long-tailed mackinaws like you see in the cigarette ads—and he unsnapped the tie-down on his gun. It was a little thing, just a motion."

"Bill told me a number of times, somebody's going to get killed," recalled Thiessen. "He knew there were people out there who could do it and that sooner or later it was going to happen. He said the state of Idaho's been lucky."

Though Pogue felt the need for game wardens to carry a handgun, he relegated them to second place behind the force of personality. He never trained to score high at the six-month certification shoots. For one thing, he had no sight in his right eye and was not a good pistol shot. More fundamentally, he wasn't interested in guns. "He preached gun safety to me like you wouldn't believe," said Steve Pogue, and there were always a few rifles around the house, work weapons. But he didn't collect guns the way his brother, a competition marksman, and many people in Idaho and Nevada do. One rifle in particular, which Eddie custom-built as a gift with a long scope and heavy barrel, stood fallow in Bill Pogue's house. It was a beautiful, precision-made piece that could knock a rock chuck over at three hundred yards. But during the six years he possessed the rifle, Pogue shot less than a box of shells through it, most of them at a rifle range. "Bill felt badly about never having shot that rifle," Thiessen commented. "He loved his brother dearly, but he knew what the rifle was built for and he didn't want to shoot it." The reason was simple. Pogue had quit killing animals.

Bill Pogue had never been much of a hunter, but now people began to notice that when he went with friends to the Owyhee, he'd carry a rifle but not shoot it. When Eddie went to Garden Valley during the cougar season, his brother retreated to the Longhorn to play pitch. "He hated to kill anything," said Sterling Alley. "I remember one morning there was a live deer down in the road. The cats and coyotes had really worked it, it was all tore up. And I said to Bill, 'Shoot the damn thing.' 'Ah well,' he says, 'he might live.' It was the middle of winter and the snow was deep and there wasn't a damn thing to eat. There was no way he was going to live. But Bill didn't want to kill it."

Thiessen remembers: "He said to me, 'Jerry, there isn't anything that I'd rather see dead than alive.'" He still believed that game should be harvested by legitimate outdoorsmen just as firmly as he believed that poachers were death, death on the herds, death on the wilderness. But he was no longer young. Only the people closest to him saw the change. His brother noticed. "I think he finally discovered that he wasn't going to be able to catch every poacher that was out there and every son of a bitch that was trying to take one of his animals. He mellowed, slowed down, started spending more time with his family."

Around his fiftieth birthday, Pogue stopped in at the art gallery and chatted with its owner, Gloria Brown. "It really bothered him. He said he was getting old enough to be a grandfather now." A few months later, he visited again, this time in search of the original of his favorite drawing, "Mountain Man." This was a picture of a mountain man, bearded, buckskinned, and with his hair in pigtails, touching a strand of barbwire. As he looks into the inner gut of the twentieth century—at the roadmakers, the fence builders, the subdividers—a touch of resignation illuminates the man's eyes. "He told me he had once encountered this character," Brown recalled. In fact, the mountain man whispered in his mirror every time he looked. Pogue never quit longing for simpler, rugged times when he might have been a trapper or cowhand, closer somehow to the god in the wind and forest.

Then he was gone. Bull Camp swallowed him. It was on

the news, in the papers. And next day, Brown's Gallery sold every last print Pogue had submitted. When the reward fund started, one drawing was offered in a limited-edition memorial sale at $100 per print. The proceeds were to go toward capturing his killer. The drawing was "Mountain Man."

# Chapter 6

**T**HE lawmen alone held faith that Dallas would be run to earth, but not anytime soon, and probably not alive. Dallas had sworn, said Irene Fischer, "that if he was caught he'd shoot it out, and that if it got down to his last shell, he'd shoot himself before he'd be taken." There was no reason to doubt that samurai bravado, although edges of the image had begun to soften. What in the first weeks had stalked the public's geography as a mountain man, now took on smaller dimensions, at least for lawmen like Tim Nettleton. "When it first started, Claude was a wild-eyed trapper, all that bullshit that was in the paper. I thought when this first happened," Nettleton said, "that Dallas had been born and raised here. But then I started talking to people who'd known Claude. It took me about three months to put him in a little better perspective. I learned that he'd been raised in Ohio and didn't come out here until he was eighteen, and he was thirty now . . . in ten years you don't get that kind of experience. He was still an outsider to the land itself. I believe that he was tough, physically tough. But he also had a soft spot in his heart. He was soft enough to where he packed a rubber mattress [a foam pad] with him."

Confirming the soft spot, another lawman pointed out, "He had people bring him cookies." "He was too clean, too neat," said Steve Bishop, Humboldt County's undersheriff, who had known Dallas while trucking Paradise cattle. "I started to feel that maybe he wasn't that much of a mountain man." The details were small, almost picayune, but they served to reduce the myth to human proportions. The man had strengths, but he had weaknesses, too. Somewhere the trapper would display an Achilles heel. "We'll get him eventually," Nettleton said ten months into the manhunt. "It may take a year or two, but we'll get him. From the very beginning we were looking at a long battle."

The sheriff studied Dallas, incorporating bits and pieces into a familiar desert mosaic. "Just about anybody who spends one winter alone, and everybody who spends two winters and more up there alone on that mountain is odd," he observed. "The rest of their life, they're odd, marked. Those kind of people are more perceptive about certain things, and they're also more protective than ordinary people. Claude was that way."

Nettleton explored Dallas's literature on weaponry and shooting, too, for clues to his frame of mind. He even delved into fiction, as much as he could stomach at any rate. "Claude read a lot of Louis L'Amour, just devoured him, so I tried to read him," he said. "But I couldn't stand him." Dallas began to make more sense. He was no mad trapper, just a dreamer, what

Nettleton called a "romantic paranoid" who had read too many cowboy novels and paramilitary manuals. "I think that between reading Louis L'Amour and listening to George Nielsen's bullshit," he remarked, "that's what led Claude up to Bull Camp." Even while deriding the exaggerations and probing the trapper's flaws and vulnerabilities, Nettleton respected his prey. Searching farther afield, he found a number of remarkable parallels between his trapper at large and another trapper, Albert Johnson, the subject of *The Mad Trapper of Rat River* by Dick North. Following a trapping dispute nearly mirroring the one Dallas had with Ed Carlin at Bull Camp, the Canadian hermit was contacted at his Rat River cabin by Canadian Mounties in January 1932. He gunned down one lawman and escaped on snowshoes. Not a very large man, about the size of Dallas, Johnson astounded even the rugged Mounties by carrying a gigantic backpack over the Richardson Mountain Range in midwinter. After a brutally extended chase and with the aid of an airplane, Johnson was finally surrounded on the ice-locked Eagle River, a tributary of the Mackenzie River. News accounts had predicted that the mysterious "mad trapper" would go down in a blaze of gunfire, and he did . . . but not before a bullet exploded a pocketful of shotgun shells, tearing away most of his hip, and not before he killed his main pursuer.

Nettleton collected every last splinter and bump, entering the data—in lieu of a computer—into manila folders stacked in a cardboard box. In his office vault were stored all seventeen of Dallas's guns, plus gear that included his foam ground pad. He passed along to the FBI and Frank Weston's office in Winnemucca what he judged relevant to them, and in turn received what they considered pertinent to him. He marshaled public attention (if not always opinion) by feeding newspaper and magazine journalists newsy scraps of information, just enough with each interview to give writers a fresh lead for a cold story. In the ION region, Claude Dallas became a small cottage industry; with the aid of Nettleton's leaks, new articles cannibalized old articles. Owyhee County's prosecuting attorney, Clayton Anderson, tried to suppress the sheriff's interviews and block the media's access to him, but Nettleton had a simple philosophy: "You can't cook the stew until you catch the rabbit." He defied Anderson. "I told him, this thing's already a mess and I'm going to make it more of a mess. We've got to use the press. They can spread this thing a lot better than we can. I said let me play the dumb bumpkin sheriff, let me just play it to the hilt. I'll set right here and they can write whatever they want about me. I'll just keep things flowing out to keep this thing going." With his hand-tooled boots and a gold and silver belt buckle the size of his Chesterfield Kings box, he gave the press a sheriff to match the outlaw.

The returns were tangible, if small. Examining a photograph in one magazine article about Dallas, Nettleton established once and for all that his quarry had a small but distinguishing mole on his left cheekbone. Because of the constant publicity, tip-offs continued to pour in. "It's a bad time to be wearing a beard," Steve Bishop observed in response to a flood of calls. Most tips amounted to nothing. But some gave meat to the hunt, as when a northern Idaho merchant reported that Dallas had purchased a green, eighteen-foot Kelvar canoe and an AR-15 rifle in October 1980, and authorities theorized he may have concealed the canoe across the Canadian border.

In early March, Canadian customs officials made a positive confirmation of a bearded man matching Dallas's description. He was sighted in the Yukon Territory, then at a gas station in Glenallen, Alaska, again in Nenana, then again at Tok Junction, where the Alcan Highway forks to Fairbanks or Anchorage. At last he was arrested in an Anchorage grocery store, fingerprinted . . . and released, the wrong man. Nevertheless, said Nettleton, "Alaska is my own favorite, personally. All I'll guarantee is that [Dallas is] in the northern half of the Western Hemisphere. I don't think he's in South America . . . yet." The Latin Hemisphere was not out of the question. There were reports that Dallas could speak fluent Spanish. He got along with the migrant workers who were hired and busted regularly on local farms. And one acquaintance swore Dallas had even spent time in a hellish pit in a Mexican jail.

"I'm confident Claude is traveling around the world and getting along fine," said Cortland Nielsen. "But he's got a conscience. So finally it'll hit him too much, and he'll figure a way to get lost, and that'll be the end. No one will ever see him again." On the contrary, prompted in good part by a growing reward fund (which ultimately totaled more than twenty thousand dollars), sightings of the outlaw were reported all across the nation.

In July a note was scribbled on a napkin in No Place Like Sam's restaurant in Auburn, Maine. A waitress found the message and Dallas was in the news again. "My name is the capital of Texas," the note declared, partly in longhand and partly printed. "I killed two wardens January 3/ Bobcat trap—out of season/ Only one person in this state can catch me/ Vermont a family/ but here I am/ You'll never get me." The capital of Texas is Austin, and the murders were committed January 5, not the third, but the waitress had seen a man wearing a floppy felt hat and "a beard like Grizzly Adams," features suspiciously similar to those in a photograph of the reward poster in *Outdoor Life*'s July edition. Nettleton didn't bite. "There's nothing in the whole story that has me excited," he said. "Claude Dallas is just not going to do something like that. He's not dumb." As if to confirm his skepticism, another bogus napkin message appeared later in Wyoming.

That same month the FBI picked up Dallas's tracks in South Dakota. Using the name Jack Chappell and an altered social security card, he had applied for work through an employment agency in Sioux Falls. The date of his application was January 27, just three weeks after the shootings at Bull Camp. Within a week the agency placed him at a steel plant, cleaning gates and assembling hinges on an assembly line. Careful to remain unassuming, he had gotten a haircut and shaved his beard. He wore a hat. "There was nothing unusual about him," said Alan Hanson, who'd rented Dallas an apartment. "He didn't want a six-month lease, which is standard, so we didn't sign one." Characteristically, Dallas kept the apartment "quite clean." Only one incident stood out, a trivial confrontation. "I had hit him accidentally with a steel gate and apologized," said Randall Curry, a fellow worker at the steel plant. "But he said it was too late for that and [cursed]." For two full months, until the last day of March, Dallas worked at the plant. Then he disappeared once again. Just before doing so, he confided to one man that he was headed for Texas. When Randall Curry saw the reward poster for Dallas in *Outdoor Life*, he notified the FBI. By that time Dallas had been gone for three months. Of this information, Nettleton did not breathe a word to the press. For the first time since finding his hollow and camp ashes at Geneva Springs, the authorities had located his trail. Hoping he would use the same alias, birth date, or social security number a second time, they kept the discovery a secret. But, as Nettleton observed, "He's not a wild-eyed, raving idiot," and Dallas never repeated the same masquerade.

Two months after Dallas left South Dakota (and still a

month before Curry tipped off the FBI), two of his brothers
suddenly moved to California, again exciting theories. Unknown to each other and based on separate tips ("We all played
the same game," said Nettleton. "When I talked to them, I
didn't spill my guts; same way when they talked to me"), the
Owyhee sheriff and the FBI began separate surveillances in
Mendocino County, where it was thought Dallas might be getting shelter from his brothers and possibly working as a lumberjack. "We were one step behind," Nettleton said later, and
then amended it, ". . . hell, three or four. We never did have a
good trail on him." Throughout the summer, while the Mendocino County sheriff's department (on Nettleton's behalf) and
the FBI watched for the trapper, Nettleton continued inter-
viewing Nevadans and cultivating contacts in Paradise Valley
and elsewhere. Every two or three weeks he would fly south,
ferrying a feed salesman "at a damn good freight and passenger
rate." Nettleton's budget had been tight to begin with, and the
Dallas case was consuming far more than its weight in tax-
payers' money. Besides helping pay for gas and maintenance
expenses, the salesman also enabled Nettleton to meet a variety
of far-flung ranchers and farmers, some of whom never real-
ized the cowboy-pilot was also the Owyhee lawman who was
hunting Dallas. "I had no other reason to be down in Nevada,
though. It was strictly Dallas."

The law had come late to mining and cattle country, often
in the form of vigilante committees. Justice was notoriously
swift. People made up their minds in a hurry, then lived with
the consequences. (One famous Victorian actor, David Belasco,
looked back upon the killings and hangings he witnessed in
Nevada as training for his stage death scenes.) Nettleton encountered vestiges of this lawless law everywhere, from folk
who insisted Dallas was innocent to those who recommended a

quick lynching once the trapper surfaced. Nettleton's own family roots in the ION region went back to the beginnings, the 1860s, and he understood ranchers' wariness in associating with the law. "You've got a bunch of ranches that were built on hard work, you've got a bunch that were built on moonshine, and you've got a bunch that were built on a fast rope [i.e., rustling]," he explained. "The fast rope is going out of business, but the moonshiners and hard workers are still here. A lot of those moonshiners were very industrious people. That was hard times [the Depression days] and it was a way of making a buck. Hell, Owyhee County made its best money when they hauled their corn out of here in bottles." In this borderland, half in and barely out beyond the days when Butch Cassidy robbed their bank in Winnemucca and was a hero all the same, poaching is still taken for granted. "To those people down there," said Nettleton, "that's not a crime. It's sort of like standing on the streets of San Francisco selling marijuana. It's a matter of local standards. You try and sell marijuana over here on the steps of the local bar and some old guy will shoot you in the tall knee."

What Dallas had done—taking deer and bobcat out of season, baiting illegally, killing wild horses, trapping cougars—evoked no criticism. Even the lawmen shrugged. Wild horses *were* a problem. Nettleton could remember his father driving six thousand head of horses off the desert to clear it for cattle grazing, "and hoping they'd all die running." Citing the dirty thirties when men fed their families with poached meat, Sheriff Weston remarked, "I believe to this day and age there's a lot of hungry people out there out of work. I believe that deer was put out there for the people. Now when you go out and kill somebody's cow, now that's wrong. It's also a felony. But when you're talking about killing a deer or a bird or a rabbit and you eat it, you don't waste it, then I really can't see getting excited over it. It's there, you're hungry, you go out and get it and eat."

Killing two game wardens was drastically different from a game violation, but as time passed and Dallas continued to elude his trackers, what shock his friends and supporters might have felt initially wore off. For many, the murders settled into a rich sediment of valid and outright courageous resistance. Self-defense was survival. Taking a stand meant not only emancipation, but existence itself. The ranchers' Sagebrush Rebellion was a case in point. With Ronald Reagan freshly ensconced in the presidential saddle and Interior Secretary James Watt wearing a cowboy hat, the tradition of fighting for what was yours seemed stronger and more necessary than ever. The BLM had grown more flexible, and legislation begun in 1978 to protect cattlemen's interests was beginning to be felt. Cattle prices still weren't "too shiny." Inflation was crushing and the American public seemed permanently bent on eating more vegetables and less beef, but in the cow counties there was a feeling of battle well done and a siege well endured. "The rules were relaxed," said Sammye Ugalde, "because the ranchers fought." In discussions of Claude Dallas, buckaroos, ranchers, farmers, and their women reiterated with conviction the need for force to vanquish bullies and giants.

"Those wardens come there to kill Claude," said Gary Rose, his friend from the Alvord Ranch. "Pogue drew his gun. You can believe it or not, but I believe it. When all this shooting started, well, it just scared Claude to death, he was defending his life, and he just kept going. It sounds gruesome, those extra shots to the head, it sounds so terrible. But you can't kill a corpse. Hell, they got in a gunfight."

"Have you ever killed a rattlesnake?" his wife, Becky, joined in. "I've been scared to death by rattlesnakes, and I'll immediately get off my horse and kill them. And after he's dead and you know darn good and well he's not going to hurt you, I still cut their heads off."

"You can't compare a rattlesnake with Bill Pogue," Gary Rose interrupted.

"You can too," said Becky Rose.

Others decided the mystifying head shots had been an act of mercy. "There was no way those wardens could have survived," said Hoyt Wilson. "There's no way you could get them out of there, and the closest hospital's a hundred miles away. And so you might as well make sure, put them out of their misery. Like with a cat in a trap." Trappers were embarrassed by the coups de grâce, which reflected on them all. People joked that the first thing to do after a car accident was pray that no trapper showed up to relieve your suffering.

Throughout the summer, Nettleton walked through a card castle of similar conjectures. "I've got a chicken over there," summarized one woman, "that if you corner it, it'll fight back." Some, like Sammye Ugalde, disapproved of the murders in one breath, and in the next would say, "Pogue was a bastard. How he never got shot before, I'll never know. I say that with a clear conscience." There was a lot of clear conscience in the ION region. Nowhere was the support stronger than in Paradise. "When this thing suddenly broke in the news and I went out there to have Sunday school," Reverend Inzer recalled, "the first thing the kids said was, 'Hope they never catch Claude.' I mean the *kids*, little old squirts in second and third grade. He was a household name." The trapper touched a distinctly, if imprecisely, political nerve, too. On one of his flights south, Nettleton trailed behind his friend, the feed salesman, into a bar in Pioche, Nevada. Out of uniform and unrecognized, the sheriff took a seat at the far end of the bar and watched the reaction as his friend stapled reward posters for Dallas on the wall. "Before long," said Nettleton, "several cowboys wandered down and started complaining about the Communist who was posting reward posters."

"A lot of people in the area told me, 'Why don't you back off and just leave him alone?'" said Sheriff Weston. "'He's one of the nicest men we've had around.' The women especially. This one woman came out to my car and said, 'Why don't you just leave him alone? He's a nice man. He opens my car door for me, he helps me with the dishes, he's just a really fine man.'" He was an appealing figure to nearly every woman who had met him, and many viewed him as a son or younger brother. ("He was sort of funny about women," observed one male friend. "There was good ones and bad ones, no in-between. Bad girls lived at, like Penny's [the Line whorehouse]. Good ones lived somewhere else. No in-between.")

"I think they sent a gunslinger up there to Bull Camp," insisted Geneva Holman, a feisty and matronly friend from Reno. "You don't travel all the way through that country to give a man a thirty-five-dollar ticket. You have something else in mind." Irene Fischer sketched on paper an elaborate vision of the moment Dallas shot Pogue: Behind and around the trap-per, like a momentary halo, shimmers a hazy saloon, and deeper in the background rise buildings and skyscrapers, the urban landscape Dallas mythically repudiated, tucked in a nar-row alley of his psyche. In the foreground spreads the desert floor, real and present. Fanning his six-shooter, Dallas stands half crouched. Fischer also painted a color portrait of Dallas on the forehead of a cow skull, basing it upon William Albert Allard's photo in *The American Cowboy* of that shy young buck-aroo who'd spent Christmas with her and Walt ten years ear-lier. One of her sketches was hung in the bar in Paradise Valley. "I'm very sorry for what he done," she said, "sorry because we'll never see him again. I hope he never gets caught for the simple reason I don't think Claude will ever be taken alive. I wouldn't want him to kill anyone else, and I wouldn't want them to kill him. And I wouldn't want him to end up killing himself."

The murders had polarized Paradise Valley. "No one walked the middle of the road," said Frankie Zabala, the schoolteacher. Moderate opinion came in two varieties, that Dallas had never pulled a trigger, and that bureaucrats had driven the trapper to desperation. "I'm being hard-nosed," said Liz Chabot, expressing the first variety. "I still don't think we've got the whole story on this. I don't think we ever will. There were two people there [Dallas and Stevens]. And they never found the murder weapon, so they don't have the ballistics to go on."

"I think that Claude would lie, deliberately lie to save a friend," added Frankie Zabala.

"Stevens was his friend," Chabot agreed, "and he had those little kids."

"That's right," said Zabala. "He was going to take the rap anyway. So he was going to take it for everything." Murder was bad, they agreed. But Claude wasn't. Propelled by friendship and his code of biting the bullet, the trapper had gallantly sacrificed himself for a lesser man. No less ritual and tragic an interpretation was the widespread view that a man of the earth had been pushed to violence by agencies, agents, and those henhouse regulations and rules. The men who tendered this view were often those who had lost land, money, or livelihoods to the advancing times, men like Harold Chapin, the mustanger whose wild horses were now protected by federal law.

"I think the bureaucracy contributed to Claude's frame of mind," he said. "I'll always believe that. The way the regulations are set up is what caused that to happen." As proof, Chapin referred to a deer shoot in Paradise Valley. A large deer herd off the mountain had been plundering ranchers' hay, and in response to complaints, Nevada Fish and Game authorized an out-of-season hunt. It was carefully controlled. Hunters were selected by lottery and could use only shotguns due to the proximity of homes. In no time at all, it became a local scandal. Not only were no licenses issued to Paradise Valley residents, but a hundred dead and wounded deer lay where they fell. Many, torn by shotgun blasts, escaped to suffer on the mountain. "Basically it was the same deer herd Claude took his deer from [at Bull Camp]," said Chapin. "They [Fish and Game] were down at this end of the mountain shootin' em and lettin' em lay. And they're going to hang somebody for eatin' one up on that end? Now to me," he concluded somberly, "that's the bureaucracy itself." The deer shoot was conducted shortly before Dallas killed the game wardens, an event that later struck locals as one more absurdity on the heap.

"They weren't bad citizens," insisted Frank Nenzel, an FBI agent on the Dallas case. "They were just confused citizens." Not many actively thwarted the manhunt, but few actively assisted it. The lawmen didn't begrudge that refusal. "I'll tell you what about a lot of people in Paradise," Nettleton said. "When you shake their hand, you don't need a contract afterwards. Their word's good. They treat a stranger just like they treat one of their own. And a lot of them still take Claude at his face value. I don't have hard feelings for the people who were friends with him and who look me in the eye and say go to hell." Not all of the Paradise ranchers were saying go to hell, though. On his various trips to Humboldt County, Nettleton made contact with the few who were willing to help, and nursed along their cooperation. "I had some people down there who were downright rude to me if I walked in the bar," he said. "But they'd let me know they weren't for Claude. They didn't like what he'd done." It took time, but eventually he developed informants. "I knew every time Frank Gavica [one of Dallas's friends] took a shit down in Paradise."

The seasons turned. Winter came. "Nothing would surprise me about Dallas," Nettleton told the press. "He could be
on a ship at sea or be a bank teller in New York." They had
given up on finding Pogue's remains. That was a continuing
point of anguish for the family. "Someday, some way, maybe
he'll be man enough to let us give Bill Pogue a decent burial,"
the sheriff challenged publicly. A year and five days after the
Bull Camp killings, he shrugged and said, "About all I can say
. . . is that Claude Dallas is still alive."

Not only was Dallas alive, he was back in Nevada. He had
come full circle and returned. Some people knew, most didn't,
but the rumor spread. "If he come in off the desert," his old
friend Cortland Nielsen anticipated one day, "first thing I'd do
is have him sit down and give him cheese and booze, and hell,
if I had a steak . . ." There were suddenly stories that men were
leaving pickup trucks in the desert for him full of gas, key in the
ignition, provisions on the seat. One afternoon, while "pushing
church" a hundred miles from Paradise, Reverend Inzer entered a bar with his wife. As they seated themselves at a table,
the reverend looked around and, to his astonishment and de-
light, spied the fugitive. Dallas's long hair was cropped, but
otherwise it was that same "common recluse" Inzer had long
admired. "Honey," Inzer whispered to his wife. "You say you
never met this Claude Dallas fella. Well, you just walk to the
bathroom and he's sitting right there at the bar." After complet-
ing her circuit, Mrs. Inzer rejoined her husband and the two of
them "just died laughing." For while he sat there with his drink,
the trapper was leisurely contemplating a wanted poster stapled to the wall offering up to twenty thousand dollars for his
capture. Everyone in the bar had seen it, and they knew Dallas
was among them. But no one called the sheriff. To the contrary, Inzer related, "A man walked up to me one day and said,

'Reverend, do you have contact with Claude Dallas?' I said, 'Well, I might and I might not. Not with intent, but I might run into him.' And this fella hands me a hundred-dollar bill and says, 'Give this to him. And tell him if he shoots one more game warden I'll give him another.'"

Like Ulysses returned, Dallas quietly visited old friends and locations throughout northern Nevada. Bull Camp was scarcely a dot on a map, but now it was the birthplace of a legacy. Roughly a year had passed and still the trapper was free, charmed and holding true to his theater. He wintered on the mountain, trapping, hunting, and generally lying low. Lawmen suspected he was somewhere in the ION region, but could only prove where he wasn't. Rumors exulted that he was better armed than ever. Eddie Pogue heard that Dallas had a cache of weapons near Fallon, Nevada, and with the FBI, flew back and forth in futile search of it. Other rumors had it that he had practiced shooting down helicopters, just like Kirk Douglas in *Lonely Are the Brave*. Everyone agreed. He was unafraid. He was out there, bold. He was among them, but no one knew precisely where next. Cynically the lawmen waited for human nature to take over. "I've been around law long enough," said Eddie Pogue, "to know that a guy like Dallas can lose a lot of friends because of cold cash."

When a tip came, Eddie Pogue was the one to receive it on the phone one January night in Bakersfield, California. "A woman asked me if I was still interested in catching Dallas," Pogue related. "I assured her I was. She asked me if she could be paid the reward money and still remain anonymous. I assured her she could. She knew a lot about me. She knew who I'd contacted, where I'd been, even where I'd stayed. She told me, 'You come to Winnemucca and stay in the same motel you usually stay in, in the same room you usually stay in. I know where Dallas is right now. I'll contact you Saturday night at six o'clock.'"

Tempted to carry through the rendezvous alone, as he had before in his private vendetta, Pogue couldn't help but feel that this time it was a setup. He communicated the details to the FBI, who staked out the motel. At six o'clock on Saturday night, Pogue was sitting in his motel room, composed, eager to break his quest from its merry-go-round of false leads and frustration. All night long he waited for the woman to contact him. But she never showed up. He waited through dawn and then returned to Bakersfield 570 miles away. There the woman called him again.

Her husband had caused trouble, she explained, but she would communicate the fugitive's location at some other time. "She never did," said Pogue. "And after that I started getting phone calls in the middle of the night. 'Keep out of Nevada or you'll get your ass killed.'" It was then that the lawmen figured Dallas was not much longer for sagebrush country.

# Chapter 7

**B**Y trapper's logic, it was the season to move, to exit the Country. The weather was warming, pelts were on the rub, and spring was a fine, rich odor. The willows showed buds and soon Calico Mountain (relabeled Capital Peak by the government) would erupt with colors. It was that season when enormous, tall winds rip at the topsoil, when ranchers prepare to move their cattle to the mountain, and everywhere the animals are in motion. Turn on your pivot sprinklers and you might flush out a coyote bitch and her dozen pups. At night, owls with gigantic wingspans jumped through the blackness, launched suddenly from the corrugated roads with mice or lanky jackrabbits in claw. Quail and chukars pottered about like rapid professors. The land was alive again. It seemed likely

Dallas would surface on his way to somewhere else, for like the animals he was a creature of pattern. It was like him to winter remote in the outback. It was like him, come spring, to break loose of the wilderness and find work on a ranch or farm or just visit some friends. The lawmen watched.

He wasn't invisible. Certainly he wasn't anonymous. But Dallas seemed to carry with him a shield, an invulnerability some would call plain, cunning luck. He could walk into a bar and stare stone-faced into the eyes of his own wanted poster, and no alarm sounded, no deputies sprouted from the earth. People gave him money and food; they sheltered him, loaned him their trucks, celebrated his deed. Many who frowned on the murders, celebrated just the same, preferring to see (or hear of) him free. He was a benign spirit, the star-crossed picture-book outlaw. His teeth were undecayed, there was no syphilis in his brain, no misanthropy scrawled upon his square, bespectacled face. He wasn't tattooed like the drifter from Hollywood who'd murdered an entire Pershing County family in their home (marked to no effect with a sign warning "This Property Protected by Winchester"). Nor was he misshapen like the killer hermit Bristlewolf. Young and strong, Dallas was a wise, shy cowboy. Somewhere out beyond, cautious as a cougar, he was sniffing the dawn air. When his time came, he had announced, he would be ready. He would not shrink from the task. That was understood. "If you're a trapper and hunter and you live with life and death the way he did," said Hoyt Wilson, "you've got a pretty good idea that you're not going to last forever." Poised in a frontiersman's dream, he had weaponry and skills, and the day-to-day paranoia had one exquisite, all-consuming purpose: survival.

He was proof that the obsolete West was alive and vital, moreover that it was canny and intelligent. For ninety years,

ever since the Census Bureau officially declared the frontier a
dead issue, the cowboy had been yodeling his own swan song,
with all America for a chorus. No book about the West was
complete without a Boot Hill nod to the bygone saddle tramp.
No cowboy mounted his air-conditioned pickup who didn't
reckon his ancestors had had it better, clearer, purer. Modern-
day ranchers and cowboys love to debunk their own myths just
as fervently as they hate to see outsiders not believe in them.
With Dallas at large and repeatedly outwitting the twentieth
century, though, there was no need for the debunking. The
frontier mythology was real and intact. If Claude Dallas could
find hiding places on the desert, then so could their faith in the
old days. He seemed to confirm that what had been good
enough in the boots-and-saddles era was plenty good enough
today.

Outside the cow counties, too, his outlaw reputation held.
Dallas couldn't help but notice. One early morning in northern
California while washing in a cold stream, he was startled by
two hikers walking down an obscure trail. He could see by their
wide eyes that they had recognized him. Remarking on the fine
morning, they edged backward, then turned around and slowly
marched back up the trail as if all were well and normal. The
moment they moved out of sight, Dallas raced through the
trees to a ridgetop in time to spot them galloping for safety
down the opposite valley. For a spell, he worked and lived in
the forests of Mendocino County, California, sheltered by his
brothers. His journey had described a huge loop east and south
through the nation, from Paradise to Sioux Falls, and from
there to the Great Lakes region, Texas, and California. Traveling mainly by bus, every leg had been threatened by discovery.
In one city, he told friends, he had entered a flophouse lobby
only to find himself surrounded by policemen. Rather than

make himself more conspicuous by turning to run, he had bra-
zened his way to the front desk and checked into a room. All
night long he shook in his boots. Next morning he learned that
the police had been investigating the murder of a sailor in a
neighboring room.

What little respect he had for the law eroded further as he
moved south to Texas and onward. The FBI's professionalism
continued to be an estimable threat to his freedom. But small-
town cops were corrupt, ignorant, and parochial, almost to a
man morally halt. He told of one incident. When a semi truck
filled with television sets overturned one night, every cop
within a hundred miles went home with a brand-new set. Another night, while sleeping in a brush pile beneath a bridge, he
woke to the sounds of policemen bullying a drunk. While he
lay hiding, they forced the drunk to jump from the bridge,
which snapped both the man's legs. "When you're a down-and-
outer," Dallas concluded, "boy, you're in big trouble." He was in
big trouble. He had failed to make the FBI's Ten Most Wanted
list, but that did nothing to diminish the danger of arrest. In
Texas, he told friends, a bus carrying him and one other passenger was stopped at a roadblock. Brandishing a tattered library card bearing another man's name, Dallas barely managed
to bluff his way clear. His was a terrain of continual close calls,
good luck, and Odyssean cunning.

Silence, which had long worked well for Dallas, provided
fertile soil for additional rumors. One gleeful tale had him
bearding the lion in its den by cutting trees for the BLM in
Austin, Nevada. Another related how the fugitive had been
arrested on a drunk charge in New Mexico and then released.
Only a week later, when his fingerprints were checked, went
the story, did the lawmen realize they had unwittingly arrested
and freed him. He used at least three aliases, one as a laborer in

Sioux Falls, one borrowed from the old, discarded library card in Texas, and one taken from a lumberjack in northern California.

In the summer of 1979, Dallas and his brother Stuart had lived in a cabin outside Redway, California, stripping bark from felled trees on a contract basis. A burly lumberjack named Randy Conrad had met the two brothers, and the following year hired Stuart as a landing man. Lumberjacking is seasonal in Mendocino County, running from May through October, seventy to eighty hours a week. When a wire pierced Stuart Dallas's pupil, he nearly lost his eye but continued the trade. In the summer of 1981, while Claude was still at large, two more Dallas boys suddenly showed up in Fort Bragg looking for work, and Conrad hired them on as a landing man and choker setter. Both Nettleton and the FBI noted this clustering of Dallas males and, on the presumption there was fire within the smoke, inserted surveillance teams. "I heard there were people working on our crew who were poking around," said Conrad. "The Dallas brothers weren't bothered by it, though. They laughed and joked about it." Aware that the area was being monitored, Dallas left the circle of his brothers and retreated at last to the old sanctuary of Nevada. With him he took a small set of identification papers borrowed in some fashion from Randy Conrad. In the packet of papers were Conrad's birth certificate, a social security card, two insurance cards, a Veterans Administration card, and an old snapshot of his wife and baby boy. It was a careful selection. None bore an image of Conrad, nor apparently listed the lumberjack's dimensions: six feet and 230 pounds. Conrad didn't mind. "No better'n I knew him than I'd give him a million dollars and trust him with it," he vouched for Claude.

Back in Nevada by September 1981, Dallas had plenty of

time to gather together nearly 140 traps (some stamped with
U.S. government initials) before pelts came into prime. The
winter solstice came and went, cats began rubbing, and then it
was time to move on. He had his eye on Alaska, territory and a
life-style that were familiar and remote. He collected his possessions—the traps, five handguns and three rifles, and a duffel
bag containing his false identification, a tube of hair coloring,
and two books: *The Criminal Use of False Identification* and *The
Paper Trip: A New You Through New ID.* Prepared to sink into
the wilderness once again, deeper and longer and never to be
heard from again this time, he descended into Paradise for one
final visitation.

On a Wednesday night in mid-April, FBI agents from
Reno and Boise met with Tim Nettleton and Idaho State Investigator Harry Capaul at the Thunderbird Motel in Winnemucca. Though they were meeting in the heart of Humboldt
County, they neglected to invite Sheriff Weston or any of his
deputies. "We didn't intend to slight the Humboldt County
sheriff's office," said FBI Agent Frank Nenzel. There was a
feeling, however, that Weston's office was porous and that information had a way of moving out to Paradise. Besides, there
was nothing extraordinary about the meeting. "We got together," said Nenzel, "to kick around what was going on and to
enhance the investigation." There was a consensus that Dallas
was nearby and in motion, vulnerable. "It was just a gut feeling," said Nettleton. "He was somewhere around, ready to do
something. Spring was starting to break and he almost had to
come down to Paradise and contact some of his friends before
leaving."
    Though professing a leaning toward intuitive reasoning,
Nettleton's feeling was based on more than his gut. The people

of Paradise were beginning to talk, and through his informants, the sheriff was listening. "A lot was based on comments being made by Danny Martinez (a local buckaroo) and George Nielsen that Dallas was too smart for us. And some of it was that Frank Gavica was talking about him, and it just wasn't like the old bastard." Martinez, Nielsen, and Gavica were all considered prime candidates for a visit, and they and several others were being watched both formally and unofficially. (Unknown to the FBI, Eddie Pogue periodically staked out Nielsen's bar at night.) In addition, a new candidate had quite literally entered the picture. Nettleton had obtained a group photograph from Jim Stevens that was taken on the festive caravan to Bull Camp the year before. Each figure in the color snapshot had been identified and located. But in late March 1982, almost magically, one more figure had surfaced on the photo. His image had always been there, of course, a thin, erect man in a Levi jacket, but somehow he had silently slipped their attention. "Hell," said Nettleton, "we'd never identified this one guy. We didn't know anything about him. I hadn't developed any informants around him." Working quickly, they remedied the oversight. The mystery man was a fence builder named Craig Carver. Fully as reclusive as Claude Dallas, Carver was a thirty-five-year-old ex-Marine and Vietnam veteran who lived alone on a blank stretch of desert locals had dubbed Poverty Flats. His badly weathered trailer was perched on the edge of a junkyard of old and destroyed cars and trucks. Shy and dependable, Carver stuttered and minded his own business, and, though considered odd, he was well liked. Throughout the day he would be gone, setting posts and stretching barbwire for Paradise ranchers, then at dusk people would see him driving one of his old trucks home at a snail's pace, five or ten miles an hour. Once identified, he was added to the list of friends Dallas might visit. The meeting lasted until one in the morning ("We didn't even have to play the nickel slot machines that time," joked Nettleton). Next morning the lawmen went their separate ways. After all the conjectures had been tendered and notes compared, they were still no closer to capturing Dallas. Unless someone informed on the trapper, waiting and watching were their sole options. Only a day or two passed.

Before dawn, in that cobalt-blue span called the wolf's hour, Nettleton was awakend by a phone call from the FBI. An informant had called their office shortly after their Winnemucca meeting, and had offered some promising details. It was 5:00 A.M. on a Sunday morning, and by the sheriff's own estimate there had been a thousand tips and leads. A bare handful had been more than fool's gold. This time, however, the excitement seemed justified. Nearly sixteen months into the manhunt, Dallas had been sighted just a few miles from the place he had disappeared on Sand Pass Road. According to their informant, Dallas was back almost precisely to the point at which he had exited. Out on Poverty Flats, Craig Carver had a guest. FBI SWAT teams were being called up from three states, aircraft had been arranged, spotters were being posted on a mountainside overlooking Carver's hovel. They were going to raid the site. Did the sheriff care to participate?

By nine o'clock Nettleton was standing in a crowded room at the Thunderbird Motel, 250 miles south of Murphy. The FBI SWAT team from Boise, composed of four or five special agents, had already assembled there, and other lawmen were arriving by the minute. It was a diverse group: state investigators, FBI agents, the Owyhee sheriff and his deputy, a Winnemucca policeman, a police chief from Homedale, Idaho, and even an Idaho state trooper who had been a friend of

Pogue's and had long ago petitioned, "When they go to catch Claude Dallas, whenever and wherever, you take me with you." Conspicuously absent from the swelling congregation was a single representative of the Humboldt County sheriff's office, which had jurisdiction in Paradise. On top of the fear that someone in Weston's office might relay news of the raiding party to Paradise, local infighting had further injured confidence in the department. That Weston and his crew were out in the cold was embarrassingly obvious and, thought Nettleton, unfair. Weston had carried the ball efficiently enough, and his undersheriff, Stan Rorex, had spent hundreds of hours searching for Dallas and Pogue's body, and Steve Bishop had been a vital ambassador to the various law agencies. They had been competent, if not as aggressive as some might have wanted. Raising these points, Nettleton got them to include Weston.

There had been a burglary at a mine in the Sheldon National Antelope Range 120 miles northwest, and Stan Rorex was just approaching the scene when the dispatcher contacted him at noon. Weston's voice interrupted, urgent and alarmingly curt. "Forget the burglary," he ordered. "Get back to Winnemucca by one-thirty." When Weston refused to describe the emergency over the airwaves, Rorex deduced that some disaster had stricken his wife and children. He had left them roofing their new house that morning. "And all I could think of was that one of my kids had fallen off and they wanted to break it to me in person. The oil went out of my vehicle, the water went out of it. But I made it to Winnemucca in time. I ran into the office and said, 'What the hell?' Frank was there. 'We got Dallas,' he said. 'Let's get down to the Thunderbird.' We drove down and everybody was in the motel room. Tim Nettleton, FBI, all these guys carrying automatic weapons, carrying fatigues to put on. It was like a madhouse."

The team leaders had located where Craig Carver's property lay and had begun planning the raid, but they were using
old road maps that showed no topographical features. From
the back of his Blazer, where he kept an entire set of the region's USGS maps, Rorex brought in a more current overview
of the countryside. As the afternoon wore on, the motel room
grew more and more crowded with men and weapons. Besides
a menagerie of handguns, there were shotguns, M16s, M1s,
and a submachine gun. It was two o'clock before the four pilots
arrived, two in a two-engine airplane to be used for communi-
cations and spotting, and two in a Vietnam-vintage Huey helicopter from the San Francisco base. A SWAT team from the
Butte FBI office arrived, and still more men and firepower were
expected. If Dallas was really there at Poverty Flats, they meant
to take him.

Since shortly after sunrise, two local officers had been
tucked away up on a flat hilltop near the butt of the Santa Rosa
Range, observing Carver's place three quarters of a mile distant
through a 25-power telescope. There had been little movement
except for a single figure, identity unknown, who had been
tinkering with the engine of a white flatbed truck throughout
the afternoon. Now and then he would drive the truck around
the lot, then stop and open the hood for further work. It was a
warm day for April, though a slight wind kept the two spotters
chilly on their vantage point. They had instructions not to use
their radio for communication unless the individual started to
leave. He seemed content and busy with his backyard mechan-
ics. Still, the sun was looping lower in the sky, and if the man
below was really Claude Dallas as the informant had claimed,
then he wasn't likely to remain docile for long. Like an invitation to flight, the desert sprawled all around Poverty
Flats, sweeping into mountainous wings on the far edges.

At any moment their quarry could vanish again into that region where nothing stands higher than a man's belly unless planted or built by men. Looking eastward toward the sprawled ranches of Paradise, settlements were clearly marked by islands of abruptly tall elms and poplars imported by homesteaders. Except for those archipelagos and the sparse line of telephone poles and power lines, the rest was sagebrush and greasewood. Here and there a string of cows meandered, and every few minutes whirlwinds would touch down, coiling fine dust hundreds of feet into the air. The dust was so dry it smoked when you spit on it. Sometimes a half dozen dervishes would spring out from the earth miles apart, and it would look like so many house fires, a whole valley of false alarms. On occasion a truck would originate at the base of dust, and the whirlwind would turn out to be its huge rooster tail. You could tell someone was coming by the billow of grit streaming behind. Through the long day, everyone's approach was telegraphed miles in advance. There was one exception to the signal. As the two men waited and watched at midafternoon, a pickup suddenly appeared, nearing Carver's place, moving so tediously slow—no more than three or four miles an hour— that it raised no dust. Suddenly it was just there, entering the barbwire surrounding Carver's lot and field, and a man emerged. It was impossible to identify him either. The afternoon stretched on. The Bloody Run Hills turned a darker, richer shade as the sun wheeled down. Night was Dallas's high ground. If he chose to slip away, and they had to presume he wouldn't choose to remain in Paradise, then before their eyes the fugitive was escaping once again. The informant had allowed them one 25-power peek. But the day was gone now. They had squandered their advantage, or so it seemed.

By five o'clock the small army of men had finally left the

Thunderbird Motel, but only after being joined at the last minute by a third and final SWAT team, this time from Las Vegas. "We were actually starting to move off our initial point," said Nettleton, "when they showed up. They got out of their business suits, into their fatigues." The raiding party now included nearly twenty men, the majority of whom wore khaki camouflage, the distinctive SWAT baseball caps, and toted M16s. Stan Rorex had already donned his own version of combat uniform, a bright orange jumpsuit, and had been assigned his location on one of his maps. His job, like that of the other non-SWAT officers, was to serve on the perimeters as an observer and backup. Nevertheless, he said, "I wanted a sharpshooter with me in case Dallas tried to make a getaway and came right towards me. 'No, he's not going to get away,' they said. 'You won't need anybody.'" After further consultation, Nettleton relented and assigned Rich Wills to his post, the Idaho highway patrolman who had been a friend of Pogue's. As Rorex departed with his "shotgun," he discovered that Wills had been designated a photographer and carried a camera, no more. "I asked him what he had for a weapon," said Rorex. "He said, 'Nothing.' I began to panic a little bit. My wife had given me for our anniversary a forty-four Magnum, so I gave him that with six shells. He said, 'I think we better stop and get some film, I don't have any film.' So we went and got some film and a box of shells. Then I said, 'I better go back to the office and pick up my M-One Grand.' I had armor-piercing shells for it."

Twenty minutes north of Winnemucca, the raiders began filtering into position well out of sight of the pair of men at Carver's place. The strategy hinged on each of the SWAT teams pinching off the escape routes and leaving Dallas no option but surrender or a hopeless gun battle. General opinion held that Dallas was not going to be rooted loose with less than a killing shot. "We never expected him to come without shooting," said Nettleton. Dallas was heavily armed, defiant, and, according to rumor, ready and able to shoot down a helicopter. With him, however, would die the secret of where Bill Pogue's body lay. At the mailboxes and at a yellow cattle guard marking two exits off the paved Highway 8B leading to Paradise Valley, two of the SWAT teams took up position in vehicles. They blocked the two converging dirt roads at one end. At the other end Rorex and Wills were parked in a gully to observe any unlikely effort to escape away from the highway toward the Owyhee Desert. The key to the strategy was the Huey helicopter, which contained the third SWAT team.

Overhead a faint drone marked the recon airplane circling at fifteen thousand feet, the relay link between each group of attackers. Everyone was positioned. It was six o'clock. By standing on the running board of his Blazer and looking through a pair of 50-power binoculars, Rorex could see the mass of junked cars and Carver's dilapidated trailer. A lone figure was tinkering with a truck. The other man had gone inside the trailer. "I gave Richard [Wills] the binoculars," said Rorex, "and relayed what he was seeing on the radio. It was getting closer and closer to dark. I said, 'Where's your helicopter?' Because if he took off on a run and it was dark, we'd lose him." Twenty minutes remained in the day. Jackrabbits cantered through the brush like furry grasshoppers. The cattle of Paradise lowed, and birdsong broke out intermittently.

Just as the sun dipped low to touch the rim of the Bloody Runs, the Huey helicopter sprang from the earth. It had hugged the backside of the range all the way from Winnemucca, and now it stormed up and over the mountains, thundering straight from the sun toward Carver's lot. It shot overhead past the shanty trailer at 140 knots, then banked, and a quarter mile to the east, beyond an old shed, dropped close enough to the ground to disgorge its SWAT team. Five SWAT raiders fanned out, and instantly the helicopter was aloft again, maneuvering high out of range. Dust blew with the rotor wash.

The lone man in the dirt yard instantly dropped to the ground. Circling the trailer, the helicopter emitted its siren wail, then cut it off. "All the expectations were that the door was going to explode open," said Nettleton, "and he'd be firing." When he appeared, though, it wasn't through the door. For a moment the scene was frozen. All eyes were fixed on the trailer, which seemed suddenly lifeless. Inside nothing moved.

Abruptly a man came plummeting through a glass window and screen on the side. Without checking his momentum, he rolled to his feet and dove beneath a small camper parked beside the trailer. For perhaps thirty seconds he stayed there, partially enclosed but not protected, not well enough. Assessing his poor chances between two wheels on flat dirt, he emerged from under the camper and, in a display of bravado or fatalism, straightened up and simply, calmly walked across to that old white flatbed he had been fine-tuning all day long.

If this was Claude Dallas, he was changed. His ponytail was gone, hair cut short. He still wore a beard, though it, too, was cropped down from the pictures of him taken at Bull Camp. His wire-rimmed glasses were absent, possibly lost in the window dive or hastily left in the trailer. He wore a dirty pair of combat fatigues camouflaged for jungle fighting, and a dark blue denim shirt. In his hands he carried a .30-30 lever action rifle and a revolver. Walking, not running, he made no move to surrender or to shoot, and by his actions clearly considered the desert junkyard an unfit stage for battle. Maybe he had in mind some better spot, or simply imagined escape was still possible. The desert hung on every side, *his* desert filled with hollows and hills and that deceptive flatness, laced here and there with caches of supplies. Certainly night was close. He saw a chance and took it.

The vehicles filled with other SWAT team members began bearing down on Carver's lot, trailing thick rooster tails of dirt. Dallas climbed into the truck, started it up, and headed out for the highway. When he saw the approaching vehicles on one road, he turned around to try the other road and saw that, too, was blocked. He gunned the old engine for what speed it could give and headed back into the enclosure toward the south fence. Plunging straight through, he snapped the barbwire and aimed east across the desert toward the Owyhee sanctuary.

Sequestered in his distant gulch, Rorex saw what was happening and estimated the path of escape. He jumped into his Blazer with Rich Wills. "All I could think was that if Dallas made it to these willows down the road, he'd be long gone. We'd never catch him." Rorex heard several shots and fired a few himself. Dallas powered straight across the country. On the road off to his right, Rorex kept pace and then some. Looming above the trapper as he veered through the sagebrush was a set of high-power lines. Between and beneath the lines, the Huey helicopter began diving at him, trying to force a halt.

Across terrain that can snap axles and gut tires, Dallas sped on, flung here and there five and six feet into the air. Given the advantage of a road, Rorex soon outstripped him. The helicopter dogged Dallas, circling far out front, then rocketing in toward his windshield at 130 and 140 knots, and wheeling around for another pass. On one pass, reported the pilot of the recon aircraft high overhead, blue flashes erupted from the truck. He identified it as gunfire.

"We're taking fire," the helicopter pilot confirmed. Fire was returned. From the belly of the helicopter, an FBI agent fired clip after clip at the bouncing, weaving truck. Quickly the floor was so littered with casings that the man almost slipped through the belly door. Bullets struck the truck, one piercing the driver's side of the windshield and spraying glass through the cab. Other bullets hit the door and the hood. Ahead, Rorex pulled across Dallas's path with his Blazer. Less than two minutes had passed.

The truck came to a sudden halt. An electrical connection had torn loose and the vehicle was paralyzed. Rorex was already out and behind his Blazer. "I heard more shots," he said, "and I opened up with my Reising [.45 caliber submachine gun]. But I could see my shells were falling short, so I threw it back in and got my Grand. I pumped a clip and a half into the side of his truck. I was shooting waist-high to a sitting man because I didn't want to kill him. I wanted to find that body."

The passenger door flew open and Dallas jumped out and started to run. He stumbled and fell. The leader of the SWAT teams ordered a cease-fire. They had no way of knowing yet, but Dallas had been hit in the Achilles tendon. Abandoning the truck and two handguns, he hugged the earth with his .30-30 rifle and began to crawl. He hadn't made it to the willow brake, but the sun was gone now and he had sagebrush to hide in. They had closed on him fast and he was wounded, but he still had hope.

The helicopter spotted him, then roared off to Carver's place to pick up and redeploy two squads of SWAT men. The third group pulled up within range by car, and the helicopter returned. Men were dropped into new positions. During the next ten minutes, they spread into a large horseshoe pattern, surrounding the spot in which Dallas had been sighted. Cautiously they tightened the horseshoe. It was strictly a SWAT team operation. Though Rorex wanted to participate, he was

untrained in the team's tactics and signals. He had the wrong
equipment, too, and was ordered to turn his hand-held radio
down so that Dallas couldn't hear the commands. Indeed,
Rorex was almost identified as the target himself. "Someone
said over the radio, 'Hey, there's somebody with an orange suit
on,'" said the deputy. "I radioed back quick that it was me."
Unable to resist the temptation, he began to crawl in behind
the SWAT men.

Up the road, Carver's place had emptied of lawmen. The
trailer had been secured by a SWAT team, then abandoned
when the helicopter returned to ferry help downroad. Following their role as backup personnel, the two county sheriffs,
Nettleton and Weston, were driving past the empty lot a few
minutes later when they saw a man standing alone by the
junkyard. The thought struck them both that this might be
Dallas and the man at the center of the SWAT horseshoe just a
decoy. They pulled over by the barbwire and jumped out with
shotguns. The man was ordered to put his hands in the air and
approach. In no particular hurry, he half complied. He sauntered over, but with his hands at his sides. In answer to who he
was, he replied, "Craig Carver. Who are you?"

Downroad there was nothing to be seen but sagebrush,
power lines, and several parked vehicles. Except for the sinking
sun, time had virtually stopped. Almost nothing moved. From
where he stood in the distance, said Nettleton, "It was the most
beautiful operation you've ever seen. All on radio command.
You look out there and at any one time you'd only see one man
up, never two. It was just up, run, down. Then in another
place, the next would move." All the same, Dallas was a crack
shot and this was his showdown. "Now, honest to God," swore
Nettleton, "I was standing there and I turned to an FBI man
and said, 'I wonder whose widow we're going to have to go tell

tonight.' That was my thought as they went walking in there."
The helicopter hovered overhead as men leapfrogged forward.
There was no telling where precisely Dallas had crawled to;
consequently they had to close their pattern tighter. David
Guilland, the SWAT leader, moved in with the teams. It was a
matter of ten minutes before the light failed altogether. As
it came about, only eight minutes passed before contact
was made.

According to Rorex, the circle of SWAT members actually
missed Dallas. "He could have wiped out six FBI agents because they'd run right past him." As the teams searched,
sweeping toward a logical center, Guilland was standing up
when a voice addressed his back from a dozen yards away.
"Hey," he heard. "Don't shoot. I'm over here." Guilland spun
around. "I observed a man lying flat on his back, with his
elbows and hands above his waist," said Guilland. "It was
Claude Dallas." They had caught their man.

Beside him lay a lever action rifle, fully loaded. That he had
allowed himself to be captured astonished the lawmen. He had
a weapon, night was on, and the SWAT teams' perimeter
had possibly passed right beyond him. He might have crawled
off. At the very least, he had targets. "I think he saw an opportunity there that he didn't think we'd give him," said Nettleton,
"and he took it. When whatever it was hit his foot, he decided
he didn't want to die." Whatever the reason, Guilland owed his
life to it. Dallas had seen his fatigues and recognized him as an
FBI agent. By virtue of that alone, his respect for the FBI, the
trapper had not killed the man. Later, Dallas would claim, the
agent thanked him for not pulling the trigger.

By the time Rorex reached the gathering, Dallas was face
down in the dirt with his hands cuffed behind him. His pants
leg was wet with blood, and there was a minor yet noticeable

laceration on his forehead where broken windshield glass had struck him. On the front seat lay a .357 Magnum and a .22 revolver. The prisoner was silent but cooperative. In quick order, the helicopter landed, Dallas was loaded on and flown straight to the small hospital in Winnemucca for treatment of his wound. The emergency room was secured and the hum-drum of daily procedure evaporated in excitement as the trap-per was escorted in wearing handcuffs and trailing blood. "He was very relaxed," said Dr. Michael Stafford, the attending physician. "I can understand now why people who knew him talked about how much they liked him . . . He was very cor-dial." The wound was trivial, Dallas insisted. And indeed it was. The shrapnel was not much different from a small load of birdshot, and the wound was causing him little discomfort. Everyone in the emergency room was taken with the handsome outlaw. "Very courteous," Stafford stressed. "Very well be-haved. Very polite to the nursing staff." He was captured and in chains, but he was still Claude Dallas.

Back at Poverty Flats, the overjoyed lawmen were of a dif-ferent mind. He *had* been a legend, now he was just captured. There were even undertones of disappointment that he had betrayed his promised bravura. "It was sort of an anticlimax," said one FBI agent. "I'm sure he could do what people said he could. But I was sort of expecting Daniel Boone or someone." "I figured that he'd be tougher than that," Nettleton said. "They just outmanned, outgunned, and outmaneuvered him. He didn't walk on water or anything like that when we caught him. He was just a man." Nettleton took the debunking a step fur-ther. In explaining why Dallas had returned to Paradise, he said, "It's just like a dog that you kick in the side. He runs in a big circle and then comes back home." This was no dog, though, no ordinary fugitive. All during the manhunt, Dallas's legend had been range-fed with the frontier myths and the western tradition of defiance and self-protection. The Hollywood finish . . . with the lone, cornered cowboy leaping through a glass window with his trusty Winchester and bushwacking through the desert five feet in the air pursued by a helicopter and eighteen-man posse—that had done nothing to diminish the romance. They had caught him in the nick of time. Ten minutes, fifteen minutes more, and he would have disappeared into the sagebrush and sunset. Already Stan Rorex was claiming to have fired the bullet that had fragmented in the truck door and struck Dallas's Achilles tendon. The FBI agents posed at the rear of the truck with their rifles and flak jackets and had the deputy take a half dozen photos with his crime scene camera. And as one group of lawmen exited Paradise, their driver triumphantly clapped on the siren until they had passed that den of last-ditch admirers, Nielsen's Paradise Hill bar.

In the following days, Dallas was transferred to a Reno jail while the state of Idaho initiated extradition proceedings. The Idaho authorities were eager to get on with a demonstration of justice. All along there had been a sense of rebuke in Idaho's dealings with Nevada, from the late-night phone calls prodding Weston and his deputies to move faster and harder, to the search party of 120 "foreigners" convinced that Humboldt County was sheltering Dallas. Rebuke carried in the way Weston and Rorex were nearly excluded from the capture. There was a long-held perception in Idaho that Nevadans were mired in a tarpit of contradictions; the Silver State might be home of the archconservative Sagebrush Rebellion, but it was also wildly permissive with its brothels and gambling casinos. Tolerance and support for Dallas had been a further expression of that state's twisted, anti-Christian laissez-faire. In Idaho, the rebuke stated, there was law and order. In Idaho they had an eyewitness to the cop killings (Jim Stevens had moved to a family farm in Paul, Idaho), and Dallas was going to enjoy the state's first execution by lethal injection. Anxious about this attitude, several of the trapper's friends had already journeyed into the Owyhee Desert hoping to find the state boundary marker north, not south of Bull Camp, which would have placed jurisdiction—and the trial—in Nevada. The marker dashed their hopes.

Dallas was captured on Sunday, April 18, 1982. By Monday night, federal authorities had dropped their interstate flight charge, clearing the way for extradition. A government attorney explained that murder charges in Idaho took precedence over the federal fugitive charge but that, unless dropped, the federal charge would have to be tried first in Reno. The fugitive charge is commonly used to justify the FBI's participation in a case, and in this case they had captured their man. Idaho could have him. On Tuesday the prosecuting attorney for Owyhee County, Clayton Anderson, delivered an extradition request to the Idaho attorney general, and within the hour a personal courier was carrying the papers to Reno. "Certainly it was processed as quickly as we've done," said the attorney general. "I've never personally walked the papers through that way." In the face of such an enthusiastic juggernaut, Dallas waived extradition. In Owyhee County, Nettleton laid plans to take custody of the prisoner and transport him to the tiny Murphy jail.

At the same time federal authorities dropped the fugitive charge against Dallas, they also dropped their charge against Craig Carver of harboring a fugitive. "We gave it to our attorney," said Frank Nenzel, an FBI agent. "But knowing there was a lot of sympathy in the community for Dallas, it was decided

that it would do no one any good to prosecute Craig Carver."
Echoing its old reluctance to indict the Nielsens or Jim Stevens,
the district attorney in Humboldt County also dropped charges
against Carver. Two or three days before the raid, Dallas had
showed up at Carver's trailer at 2:30 in the morning and asked
to stay. He had moved 130 traps, several stretcher boards, eight
guns, and other gear into the trailer, and except for visits to the
outhouse, had stayed indoors. Exposing his sweet tooth once
again, Dallas had put in a request for some ice cream from the
store. Beyond that, Carver claimed that he had been too busy
working to talk with his guest, and during what few exchanges
they did share, that Dallas had not mentioned his fugitive status, the dead game wardens, or any of the circumstances at or
since Bull Camp. Carver had been at Bull Camp a month before the shootings; he had been a friend of Dallas's for years; he
lived in Paradise where his guest was the most famous outlaw
in recent times. But he claimed not to know the man was a
fugitive. Therefore, he couldn't knowingly have been harboring
a fugitive. Whether or not his fantastic lie was fabricated with
the authorities' help, he was released after a single night in jail.
Paradise had tweaked the nose of justice once again.

Meanwhile the lawmen's elation and bonhomie in the wake
of the capture began to suffer a gradual, wasting revision. Only
after the "clockwork" events of the capture had settled out
somewhat did Weston and Rorex see to what extent the Humboldt County sheriff's department had been snubbed. The FBI
continued to assert that their relationship with the sheriff had
been a good and professional one. But the longer Weston had
to consider the incident, the more bitter he grew. As he saw it,
his jurisdiction had been trampled upon. For beginners, he
said, "It wasn't too swift, them not telling my department about
the tip. One of my deputies went through that area [Poverty

Flats] the night before spotlighting the houses, and he went right past Carver's place. Routine. But he could very well have been shot." He resented the suspicions about his department's ability to keep a secret, and saw the inclusion of other local law officers before him as politically motivated. (In fact, he would soon lose his reelection campaign that year to James Bagwell, one of the two men who had been positioned on the mountainside for hours before Weston was even informed of the developing raid.) "The FBI were city dudes," said Weston. "They didn't know nothing about the county per se. And then they brought in those other two [Bagwell and a city policeman], and they weren't even deputized in the sheriff's department. They didn't belong out there."

Rorex was incensed, too (particularly after he lost his job following the election). Word had begun to spread that he was trigger-happy, that he had almost shot an FBI agent by mistake, and that he had been the real reason for excluding the sheriff's department. Then it began circulating that Rorex hadn't even been the man who had stopped Dallas. Someone else, it was said, had shot the trapper in the heel. "There's no way," he objected. "There was no one on that side [of the truck] to shoot but me. I know what I was shooting." Bitter, he charged privately that the FBI had contaminated evidence. "After they took Dallas away in the helicopter, I looked in the truck, and there were two handguns on the seat. Here was evidence. These guys were FBI, you know, trained in the academy and all that crap; they could be murder weapons. So what do they do? They're picking them up, loading them, unloading them. Playing with them. I came up and said, 'Don't you think that might be evidence, don't you think they should have been photographed?' 'Oh. Yeah.' And they positioned them back on the seat and said, 'Go ahead, take photographs.' I said, 'Bullshit, that's contaminated evidence.' This was their crime scene and they didn't do anything. They didn't impound the vehicle, they didn't search the area, they didn't do anything but play with the guns until I asked them about photos." And no sooner had he taken photographs of the guns, he said, than they recruited him to take their pictures. "All these FBI agents standing there with their rifles like they're on a deer hunt. Trophy shots." As far as the two lawmen were concerned, the FBI had betrayed them. "I told the FBI, any time you need something from my office from now on," said Weston, "you better go to the judge and get a court order. Otherwise you won't get it from me."

At dawn, six days after the capture, Nettleton arrived at the Washoe County jail in Reno driving an air-conditioned Winnebago trailer home in the company of four deputies and an escort car. They came with flak jackets and M16s. The appointed hour had remained a deep secret because of fears Dallas's friends might somehow complicate the transfer to Idaho. Held without bail, Dallas had kept his silence through most of the week, meeting only with Michael Donnelly, the Boise lawyer his family had hired shortly after the Bull Camp murders. He had uttered scarcely a word to anyone else. At the extradition hearings on Wednesday, he had answered the judge's questions, no more. Reporters at the proceeding had tried to elicit a comment, but Dallas refused. He had volunteered nothing whatsoever about the location of Bill Pogue's body either. He was just as taciturn when Nettleton showed up.

This was the first meeting of the two men who had entranced the ION region with their fandango. Each had performed his motions precisely, playing to the rituals as well as being led by them. Now Dallas was headed for the gallows. "He had been waiting for the moment as long as I have," said Nettleton, "but for different reasons." The trapper's ankle was fat with infection, too tender to fit in a shoe. He was shackled nevertheless. "I introduced myself," said Nettleton. "I forced him to shake my hand. I warned him of his rights, told him I was taking him back to Idaho to stand trial for the murder of two game wardens. I got him saddled up and asked him if he was going to give me any trouble. He said, 'Let's get on with it.'"

At 6:00 A.M., shackled and bellycuffed, wearing orange prison garb, Dallas was transported out to the Winnebago in a wheelchair. The thought of using an airplane had crossed Nettleton's mind. It would have cut transit time from eight hours to two or three. But he had rejected air flight as too risky and cramped. The trailer home would give Dallas room to stretch his wounded leg. More important, ground travel would provide an extra margin of safety on the four-hundred-mile journey back to Murphy. "Crossing the Owyhee Desert," Nettleton said, "there is always a chance that a fan [propeller] would quit on a plane. This isn't the kind of guy you would want that to happen with."

They drove to Winnemucca, turned north, and slipped past Paradise Hill without incident. It was a quiet ride. Dallas said nothing, declining even to select which kind of soft drink he wanted with his lunch. "We just passed the time and he just passed the time," said Nettleton, "but not with each other." On the border of Oregon and Nevada, in that rough little cowtown of McDermitt where Dallas had once boldly laid down his money belt on the gaming tables, the two-vehicle convoy had to stop and refuel. Fully aware that the outlaw was still considered a local hero, the lawmen were doubly alert to the possibility of an attack. Their prisoner noticed the concern, and Nettleton in turn noticed that. As the convoy pulled out again,

"I got this feeling that Dallas thought it was just funnier than hell, all this caution. Just a game. A while later, at the top of the hill just before starting down into Basco Station [Oregon], I turned around and looked him in the eye and said, 'Well, Claude, we're done worrying about your friends. Now we got to worry about mine.' He scooted way down," said the sheriff. "And that's the only time I saw panic in his eyes."

# Chapter 8

**R**UNNING his old-fashioned, four-cell jail with a stern benevolence, the Owyhee sheriff had a theory: "If you lock people up and treat them like animals, they'll act like animals. If you lock a dog up in a cage and kick the cage, you're going to wind up with a mean dog. Just being in jail is enough punishment for most [prisoners] without harassing them." During the brief periods he normally had them as charges, Nettleton didn't abuse or malign his prisoners. Thirty miles from the nearest grocery store, in a town with few residents and no amenities but a Coke machine, offenders and suspects often became part of the community, figuring into local gossip, providing bits of color and relief before their terms expired or they were transferred elsewhere. District judges rarely came down to Murphy, which meant prisoners had to be taxied back and forth to the neighboring county seat of Caldwell in Canyon County, a time-consuming chore that easily cost a deputy most of his day. The Dallas trial wasn't likely to be held in such a remote bend of the desert because there were no motels or restaurants to sustain a jury. And while many saw this as an open-and-shut case ("You talk to anybody around in Owyhee County," said one resident, "they've done all the judge, jury, and trial on him already"), the trial promised to be a lengthy one all the same. It was equally unlikely that the court would impose on Owyhee County the responsibility of shuttling Dallas three hours round trip each day of the trial, especially when the Canyon County jail was right there in Caldwell, and was a more contemporary facility guarded at night by five deputies (in contrast to one and a dispatcher in Murphy). That, anyway, had served as logic with the last four murder suspects in Owyhee County, all of whom had been incarcerated and tried in Caldwell. And so, even before the arrival of Claude Dallas, Nettleton had known that the celebrity outlaw would not be in his keeping for long. Defense attorneys would demand for their client better medical treatment and easier access to legal advice. Defense attorneys were also bound to object if and when Nettleton actually imported the Idaho game wardens he had invited to help guard Dallas, men not exactly disinterested in the trapper's fate. As he pulled into Murphy on Saturday afternoon and wheeled his prisoner into jail between a phalanx of deputies carrying M16s and other rifles, Nettleton had no illusions about the brevity of his guest's stay. "That was all predestined," he said. Dallas was helped into the most secure cell back in the "old" jail, and his steel door with a small window was locked shut. Stoic, Dallas continued his silence, breaking it just once for a polite request. He wanted meat with every meal.

On Sunday Eddie Pogue showed up in Murphy, full of hate for the trapper who still refused to tell where his brother's body had been dumped. By this time Nettleton counted the simmering Pogue as a personal friend, for they had shared much over the last fifteen months. Late that afternoon, the sheriff took Pogue home for dinner. Halfway through the meal, Pogue looked up and said, predictably enough, "Boy, I'd like to see that son of a bitch." Nettleton appreciated the emotion, but ignored the remark. Pogue had served fifteen years as a reserve deputy in California and knew how such improprieties sit with the public. Instead, he herded his friend over to a housewarming party at his dispatcher's house. Hard liquor was the drink. Pogue had two or three, and by his own arithmetic, Nettleton had three or four. He wasn't surprised when, somewhat later, Pogue caught his eye from across the room, came over, and in more diplomatic language renewed his request. "Sheriff," he said, "can I inspect your jail?"

Nettleton considered. He had a strict policy against harassing prisoners. But Dallas was a special case. He had murdered a good friend, and here was that friend's brother. It was a small request, and the sheriff was certain Pogue would do nothing to compromise the turn of justice. "Yeah," said Nettleton, "I think that would be appropriate." Looking over at one of his deputies, he asked, "You think you can weather just a little bit of crap if it come down?" "I guess so," said the deputy. "Then take Eddie up," the sheriff instructed. "You know the rules. Let him look at my jail."

They crossed to the courthouse and jail. Following procedure, the deputy patted Pogue down for weapons, found a handgun, and stored it and the holster in a locker. Escorted, Pogue walked back to the end of the cell block. He looked through the hole in the steel door and saw the trapper. He stared for a moment, then said, "You fucker, you're damn lucky it was them that caught you and not me."

"Who are you?" Dallas demanded.

Pogue had said his piece, though, and stalked off.

It was a bloodless, trivial reckoning, later sanitized for public consumption in the newspapers, and within twenty-four hours it cost Nettleton his control over the prisoner. It caused only a rustling of shock among newspaper readers. Eddie Pogue's late-night blustering through the steel door became part of the overall ritual, in perfect keeping with his earlier vows to "get Dallas." It was a classical fit, a rangy chord of the old revenge ballad, the ghost of vigilante justice. That it struck some folks as scandalous was just twentieth-century niceties getting the better of them. Only a fool would deny that the lines had been drawn long ago in western mythology. Outlaws had always counterpointed the law. They tempted it to descend from civilized conduct. That midnight impulse to let loose, cross the line, and hang the bastard high was a dark, familiar metaphor. Now Pogue had endured and restrained it. Sobriety, so to speak, had won out. No harm done, the incident faded rapidly. Dallas was transferred on Monday afternoon to the Canyon County jail in Caldwell, on the urban edge instead of the heart of the Owyhee Desert. That same day he was charged with two counts of first-degree murder, two felony counts of using a firearm during the commission of a crime, and a misdemeanor count of obstructing justice.

Through the hot summer, little more was seen or heard of Claude Dallas. The preliminary hearing, arraignment, and motions hearings were held in May, but except for the arraignment the outer world was permitted no view of the celebrity. The press was barred from the hearings, and to avoid prejudicing potential jurors by showing Dallas in handcuffs, the judge

ordered the second-floor hallway sealed from public view during his transport between jail cell and courtroom. Windows in
the hallway were hung with black plastic and taped shut, and
Dallas was ferried to and from the third-floor courtrooms in an
elevator. At the preliminary hearing, Pogue's best friend, Jerry
Thiessen, saw the trapper for the first time in his life. "I didn't
know how I was going to feel about Claude," he said. "He was
sitting there. I looked at the back of his head and I thought that
if I had a gun I could just walk up and shoot him. But then I
thought, you poor silly bastard, why did you do that? You're in
court now, in all this trouble. You have to go through it, we
have to go through it. You poor bastard. I didn't feel sorry for
him, just an indifference towards him. Finally I resolved that
he was not unworthy of a defense, that yes, he deserved to be
there, yes, he had rights, that yes, his attorneys were fighting to
give him the very best shake they could. Our laws require it."
Trial was set for early September in Owyhee County, then
moved to Caldwell and postponed because the judge felt extensive publicity had flattened any hopes of a fair and impartial
trial in Murphy.

During the summer, Claude Dallas, Sr., and his wife visited their son in jail. Michael Donnelly had told them to come
incognito, and so the couple flew to Reno and drove a motor
home to Caldwell. Claude Senior's anonymity was good until
they stopped for a meal and he used his credit card. The name
Claude Dallas was hardly unfamiliar. "Then I stayed in a Holi-
day Inn at the edge of Boise," said Dallas, "and my son called
for Claude Dallas. That set them up. You know, we'd registered under another name. About an hour later, two carloads of
Fish and Game men drove into the parking lot and I figured it
was time to go. I wouldn't mind meeting them face to face, all
of them. No man threatens me. I'll beat the hell out of him." It

was a disappointing trip. Seeing their son in jail was painful; on top of that they had to suffer the frustration of communicating with him through thick glass and over a telephone. They left and neither parent would return for the trial.

Meanwhile a committee of private citizens and Fish and Game officers had debated the payment of the reward. The poster had specified that up to $20,000 would be paid for information leading to the arrest *and* conviction of Claude Dallas. He had been arrested now, but not convicted. It was a fine point, and in Nettleton's opinion, "It was an error to put the part about conviction on the poster in the first place. The individual who provided the information has no control over whether he is convicted." In June, $20,500 in cash was paid to the informant by FBI agents, and a caveat was issued that the payment should not be interpreted as a presumption of guilt. An additional $1,400 remained from contributions to the reward fund, and a half dozen others who had contributed information on Dallas were considered for smaller slices of the pie. Down in Paradise, several people were nominated by local gossip as the most probable informant. Toward ferreting out the Judas, two of Dallas's friends may have gone so far as to root through one man's telephone records for evidence of calls to the FBI and through his bank statements for a sudden $20,000 windfall. Several friendships snapped over the issue, but no one could say for sure who had sold Dallas to the lawmen. Whoever it was, the authorities felt his life was only as good as his anonymity. In his county jail cell, however, Dallas was convinced it was an old friend. The man's name now occupied exactly half of an alleged, short, and ominous list of enemies to be dealt with later.

Support for Dallas remained high in Paradise. There were those ranchers who considered him a vicious punk and killer and looked for the rope to settle accounts directly. But others continued to believe in his innocence or at least in his right to defend himself. Several of his friends anxiously awaited the trial, hoping he would show remorse. For other friends, remorse had nothing to do with it. The same old stories about his Bull Camp foe, Bill Pogue, went on circulating through the valley like stubborn tumbleweed. All through the ION region the upcoming trial was anticipated as a dramatic spectacle. It was discussed at brandings and sewing bees, toasted and cursed in bars.

In mid-September, jury selection finally began in the Canyon County courthouse. Edward Lodge was the presiding judge, a careful, affable man well respected in his district. For three days the prosecution and defense teams sifted through prospective jurors. Each side rejected its full quota of ten prospective jurors, among them a man who answered that he had once extricated himself from a life-threatening situation by breaking his opponent's arm. The judge dismissed another fifteen people because they appeared to be prejudiced by the massive publicity, plus one man because of his inability to render a verdict for which death was the possible punishment. Late on Friday the seventeenth, a jury of ten women and two men was impaneled, a collection of teachers, a registered nurse, a farmer, and a publicist for the local rodeo. Dallas's lawyers, Michael Donnelly and Bill Mauk, remained concerned about the pretrial publicity, for no one had not read or heard tales about the outlaw trapper. Dallas's sympathizers had come to accept that the judge and jury were just a few bad meals and long nights between him and the needle. The state was confident. It had a glut of damaging evidence, and Dallas had nothing but a reputation for packing a .357 Magnum and dwelling in a wilderness of his own design. It was easy to be cynical. All that remained was to see how fast and hard the noose cinched tight.

Monday morning sharp, the prosecution started its long march through the evidence. They began at the beginning, with Bill Pogue in his pajamas the night he received a phone call about trappers poaching in the Owyhee Desert. The widows of Pogue and Elms each opened the doors on their last evening with their husbands, a ritually ordinary start to the tragedy. As they slipped from the witness stand, each in her turn stared hard at Dallas, who was ill at ease, each weighing him against her lost man. What she saw surprised Dee Pogue. "He was not the mountain man everyone portrayed," she said. "Everyone expected a big tough mountain man. They thought he was going to be sitting there breathing fire and he wasn't. He was an ordinary human being . . . a quiet, small, little man."

Soon enough they were finished, and with them went Dallas's discomfiture. He smiled to himself as his capture was described as a running battle, and seemed amused when the prosecution had him jumping through the trailer window and shooting at an FBI helicopter. Those instances, the prosecution asserted, demonstrated "consciousness of guilt." Guilt of Murder One. Under Clayton Anderson (Owyhee County's prosecuting attorney) and Michael Kennedy (Idaho's assistant attorney general), the Bull Camp murders were to be presented as more than a desert showdown. Dallas, they charged, had plotted an execution. Toward edifying the jury, they showed color photographs and a videotape of Michael Elms, half naked and afloat in the shallow South Fork of the Owyhee River, just as he had been found. Here were the bullet wounds in his massive torso, rope burns on his arm, and the finishing shot in the back of his skull. Time and again, the defense objected on grounds that the state's evidence was graphic and prejudicial.

Graphic, yes, Kennedy agreed. "These are not out of *Better Homes and Gardens*," he chided, ". . . this *is* a murder case."

Just as predictable, the defense strategy under Donnelly and Mauk meant to wreck the execution charge and sculpt for the jury a man of action who had been cornered by giants and circumstances and forced to fight his way clear. Deriding what he called the state's "portrait of evil," Donnelly maintained that "nearly seventy-five percent" of the prosecution's information about the murders derived from just one man, their star witness, Jim Stevens. Everyone took it for granted that the potato farmer was going to be impeached as part of the defense attack. One other man was going to have a rough go of it, too, but that also was anticipated. He was going to be savaged, slandered, and bullied. His character had to be assassinated because only by casting him into chilly disgrace could they hope to save Dallas's life. Unfortunately, that man could not be present to deflect the blows because he was dead. Photographs or videotapes of his remains would not plague the defense attorneys, for there was no body. Dallas steadfastly refused to whisper the secret. Bill Pogue had never been properly buried. But now, for the sake of his killer's life, he was going to be dug up and sacrificed all over again. The defense needed a scapegoat. By putting the dead game warden on trial for having provoked his own murder, Dallas's attorneys hoped the prosecution would be forced to defend itself, falter, and see its case collapse.

The lines were drawn. Twice a day, in the morning and then again after lunch, a hundred or more spectators queued up for entrance to the courtroom through metal detectors and deputies. With so many bodies, the courtroom was perpetually overheated. Folding chairs had to be set up and people stood in the aisles. Each day among the curious and concerned were people related to the victims or the outlaw. The widows were present and the Pogue children. Frank and Stuart Dallas were there. Eddie Pogue, acerbic and ever available to the press, attended, and his (and Bill's) sister, Peggy Sheehan, flew four thousand miles from Alaska to see justice done. "Personally," she said, "I think death is too easy of a way out. I don't think the rest of the family feels this way, but I think if he is convicted, a fitting punishment would be life imprisonment. I don't think Dallas has any social consciousness about what he did. Maybe he'd think about it if he spent the rest of his life behind bars." Not a day passed that a small knot of Fish and Game officers wasn't present, and often Nettleton dropped in for a scan. As the trial progressed, a group of a half dozen local housewives took the trapper into their collective heart. Recognizing an opportunity too good to be missed, they dubbed themselves the "Dallas Cheerleaders." They were at once a sideshow and a fan club (the unkind excoriated them as cult worshipers) who wrote peppy letters for the prisoner's entertainment. Their reward was short, sweet, and thrilling: a letter back from Claude one day. "A circus atmosphere," Fish and Game Director Jerry Conley called it. "You sit down at that trial and look at the people around you and [it's as] if they are watching some kind of soap opera. They don't appreciate the fact that it's not like . . . on television."

The courtroom audience stretched far beyond the courtroom walls, of course. It consisted of anybody who could read a newspaper or turn on a television set. For what was described as the most publicized trial in Idaho since Governor Frank Steunenberg's assassin was convicted in 1904 and sentenced to life imprisonment, the press corps was suitably exotic, ranging from writers for *Outdoor Life* to *Rolling Stone* and *Newsweek*. The wire services were there and all the local papers and *paparazzi*. Drawn to the candle flame also were numerous would-be authors, dazzled by visions of book and film contracts. One of the local television stations angered the judge by staging an off-the-cuff news poll to sample popular tastes, a chance for viewers to call in and vote for death or mercy. Vicariously tens of thousands sat in the jury box.

At the center of it all sat Dallas, quiet, focused, appearing a bit bewildered by the attention he was drawing. With his neatly trimmed beard, wire-rimmed glasses, and western-cut shirts, he had the look of a mild-mannered, scholarly rustic. "He was unlike anything most of us had ever seen," commented AP reporter John Kennedy. "He was almost a clinical specimen of a life-style none of us have ever experienced. He seemed to be the real thing." Infrequently but spectacularly, he would be further validated when the occasional comrade dropped out of the past into the Caldwell courtroom. No urban cowboys, these were shy buckaroos with stringy hair and boots of such genuine antiquity they actually laced up the front. And when they took off their outsize hats, they sported the inimitable working cowboy's tan, baked earthen up to midforehead, then suddenly pale as a white baby's bottom.

His calm and self-possession fused with his legend, made converts of nonbelievers. It didn't hurt that he was continually making somber eye contact with the jurors, a tactic basic to any good courtroom defense. Aside from the widows on the opening day of testimony, there was only one person with whom Dallas avoided eye contact, and that was the friend with a tale not even his enemies could have told. Following a week of carefully laid background, Jim Stevens took the stand and carried into the courtroom his memory of a desert trapping camp he had almost failed to reach.

"The day was real foggy," he recalled. "I was tempted to turn back several times." But as everyone gathered to hear well

knew, he hadn't. Though Stevens was in no position to appreciate it, his was grand storytelling. The details pumped like a
heartbeat. Here before them all was a creature of fate, and as he
lodged each explicit statement with the court record, the desert
tragedy took on that sort of inevitability which makes all familiar tales ring clear. All over again, he arrived at the rim overlooking a steep canyon, loaded a revolver given him by George
Nielsen, and fired it twice at a rock—the signal. All over again,
the trapper surfaced from the fogless gorge, and they greeted
each other with a banal exchange about mail and groceries,
fruit, and the pistachio pudding Stevens's wife had sent in.
With the jury at his shoulder now, the farmer descended to
camp and the slow river braiding mud on its bottom. He meandered upstream in search of arrowheads. He found one, then
heard a shout from camp, and saw Dallas standing by his tent
with two game wardens. Stevens approached. A large man
himself, he was slender next to Conley Elms. The smaller and
older warden requested the gun on Stevens's hip, emptied and
then returned it.

Dallas was being busted. Quarters of deer meat hung on
each of the steel fence posts supporting his canvas tent, and
inside Stevens had already seen two illegal bobcat hides airing
on the back wall. Stevens was embarrassed as the trapper tried
but failed to placate the older man, Bill Pogue, and so he
drifted toward the river. Still, he kept an ear on the wrangle
because after all he had driven five hours to get here and if
Dallas was going to jail, that meant driving five hours back that
afternoon. "[Pogue] sounded like a drill instructor," Stevens
said of the brewing arrest. The warden never actually shouted,
but his voice was forceful. His huge partner, Elms, emerged
from the tent with the cat hides. Stevens faced back toward the
river. "The drift of the conversation . . . was, at first I thought

they were going to take him in, then I thought they were going to cite him and just give him a ticket. Then at the end of the conversation, I thought they were going to take him in." The courtroom listened. "Claude said, 'Are you going to take me in?'" Stevens looked across the river. There was silence.

And then suddenly, "I heard either a loud shot or I heard somebody say, 'Oh no,' and there was a continuous volley of shots . . . and when I turned around and looked, Mr. Pogue was backing up and Claude was in sort of a crouched position and it looked like I could see smoke coming up against Mr. Pogue's chest . . . And when I turned around, Mr. Elms was stumbling forward and he fell right on his face off to my side." Knees bent, arm extended, Dallas held a gun. It got worse. "I couldn't believe what was happening. Claude ran into the tent and he got a rifle and he went out with the rifle and I saw him going up to Elms, and he shot both officers in the head, but I turned around, I couldn't watch." And still the horror wasn't finished.

"After the shots, I walked up and I asked him why. He said something like, 'I swore I would never be arrested again, and they had handcuffs on.' And then he looked at me and said, 'I'm sorry I got you involved in this. I've got to get rid of these bodies and you've got to help me.'" It was a long, grisly afternoon of hauling bodies on muleback, first Pogue's all the way to the rim, then Elms's, which tipped the little jenny right over, compounding the repulsion. Dallas had lit a fire near the tent to scorch bloodmarks in the earth, and as Stevens waited in shock with the mule and the tipped, bleeding corpse partway up the trail, all he could see was the thick smoke billowing up from the riverside. The trapper finally arrived, but even the two of them could not set the body back on the mule. "Claude said he was such an enormous guy . . . the only way a guy could get a guy to the top is to quarter him. And I said I couldn't do that.

And Claude says, 'There's no way I could do that either.'"
Frustrated, Dallas tied the rope to Elms's feet and tried drag-
ging the corpse downhill, but the rope simply pulled loose,
taking the boots with it. They turned Elms around, tied the
rope around his chest, and started the mule down again. This
time, the dead man's pants pulled down to his ankles, a mark-
edly grave indignity. "They kept coming down and we kept
dressing him." A final effort to load Elms on from a tiny water-
fall failed. "And finally we just gave up. Claude said, 'I'm going
to put him in the river, it's getting dark and we've got to get out
of here.'" Stevens dutifully swept at the drag marks . . . with his
hands, as ordered . . . and collected bits and pieces of clothing
torn from the corpse.

On his way back up the trail, the farmer was overtaken by
Dallas who said—and this was essential to what the state
termed the killer's "guilt of consciousness"—"'This is Murder
One for me. I didn't weight the body . . . and they'll find it in
the morning.'" The tale, as Stevens unfolded it, was a heavy
albatross around the prisoner's neck. There had been no effort
to take the downed men's pulses or to comfort them. There
had been no remorse. Dallas had been calm and serious. Over
the following twelve-hour period, he had packed bodies on
muleback, cleaned up his camp, burned evidence, concocted a
number of alibis for Stevens, commandeered vehicles, issued
instructions, buried a man, and generally demonstrated a presence of mind that was incompatible with sudden, apocalyptic
self-defense. Dallas had remarked that the shootings were justifiable homicide, but never explained why. More to the point,
he had stated, "This is Murder One for me." If the tale didn't
exactly depict calculated execution, it showed at least a matter-
of-factness that was shocking.

To make matters worse for the defense team, Stevens was a

big, decent, and articulate man of the soil, and his delivery had been as sane as it was compassionate. Quite obviously it was anguishing for him to be sitting near Dallas, giving testimony that could hurt his friend. In short, the farmer was an ordinary man who had been propelled into extraordinary circumstances through no wish or action of his own, and he had for an audience similar ordinary folk. More than an eyewitness, he was Everyman, the most dangerous enemy Dallas had just then. One way or another, the defense needed to slay the man Dallas had spared at Bull Camp. Bill Mauk opened gently. "It appears from your testimony," he started, "and correct me if I'm wrong, there are a number of things you don't recall about what happened on January fifth." Not much later, Mauk rephrased the doubt, never discourteous. "Jim," he practically apologized, "as I indicated, [our purpose] is not to embarrass you or make you feel uncomfortable. We want to make sure that you understand and the jury understands . . . I'm not trying to trip you up in any way." That said, Mauk proceeded to tangle the farmer's every step. It was a masterful impeachment.

Stevens had given six previous testimonies over the last twenty months, three of them within sixty-four hours of the murders. Mixing and matching statements from the various testimonies, Mauk hunted for inconsistencies, however trivial. On the day he had turned himself in to the authorities, Stevens had mentioned that Bill Pogue requested not only his gun but also the holster for it. Now, Stevens admitted under Mauk's goad, "I don't understand why I said that, because that didn't happen, he didn't request my holster." On sketches that located where each man had stood before and after the volley of shots, Stevens had to admit that yes, the earlier maps were slightly different from later ones. A remark he had attributed to Elms now got placed in Pogue's mouth. No single misstatement or discrepancy could reverse the fact that Stevens had been present for two murders and that Dallas had committed them. But by collecting the inconsistencies into one heap, the lawyer was able to construct a small avalanche of fallibilities. "I don't recall," said Stevens to one remark, and then to others, "I thought maybe . . . ; I believe I probably heard . . . ; I suppose he could . . . ; it could possibly have been there . . . ; I don't know . . . ; I'm not sure . . . ; like I say, I'm kind of confused on that, too . . . ; well, I'm sure I was in shock a bit." And this was the man from whom the state had obtained "nearly seventy-five percent" of its information. "We have no further questions." Mauk rested.

Playing catch-up on the redirect examination, the prosecution gave Stevens a chance to clarify his discrepancies. The farmer pointed out that he had been without sleep for forty hours at the time of his first testimony and that there were other inconsistencies besides those dangled by Mauk. "There was different things in there, like I called my son Dick, and my son is Darren. And I think there's a statement in there that I went to night school, and I don't know where that came from either." But the damage had been done. The foundations had been laid now for reasonable doubt. The man to listen to now was Claude Dallas himself. "He is the individual," Donnelly had promised on the opening day, "who can tell you what happened." Before the trapper bore witness, however, a long array of others waited to speak. Roughly a hundred pieces of state evidence, among them bobcat pelts, bullets, weapons, blood samples, and photographs, had to be pieced into the puzzle by some forty prosecution witnesses, and the defense had evidence and witnesses, too. People had waited twenty months to hear Dallas; now they waited some more.

Ever since his capture, the FBI had been contending that

Dallas had fired upon them as he jolted across the desert trying to escape. Agents claimed to have heard what sounded and looked like gunfire, in particular four blue flashes which an FBI pilot had counted. The pilot's combat record of three hundred sorties gave his claim weight, but under cross-examination another agent admitted that neither the .22 nor the .357 Magnum lying on the truck's front seat had been checked to determine if they had been fired. Both weapons were fully loaded when found, it was established. Not a single empty casing had been lying on the floor of the truck. Dallas had trained himself to shoot left-handed, and it was conceivable that he could have fired a handgun even while wrestling the truck through sagebrush and air moves, but as the defense showed, it was unlikely the handguns had been fired. It was just as unlikely that he could have levered three new rounds into his rifle and fired it one-handed. The prosecution's "consciousness of guilt" argument continued to deflate.

Matters weren't helped either when the prosecution introduced evidence demonstrating that Elms had been shot in the back. Referring to autopsy photographs, a Pocatello, Idaho, pathologist declared that the first shot to hit Elms had been in the back under his right shoulder, which then spun him around to take a second bullet in the chest, and that he probably still had been alive when the final .22 slug had entered his brain. It was an outrageous revelation, transforming a savage act into a cold-blooded one. Under questioning, though, the defense confirmed that the pathologist's opinion was based on diagrams drawn by Stevens—and Stevens had admitted to not seeing the actual shootings. His sketches had changed from time to time, and furthermore, the farmer had portrayed himself as being delirious with fear and panic immediately after the gunshots. A second pathologist was called, this one from Boise, and he baldly contradicted his colleague, stating that he was "ninety-seven percent sure" that the jagged hole in Elms's back was an exit, not an entrance wound.

Near the end of September, an Idaho criminologist further confounded the state's attempt to demonstrate that the murders had indisputably been executions. Well before Dallas had been captured, Richard Craven, a senior criminologist with Idaho Health and Welfare's forensic lab, had compared bullets from Elms's body with samples fired from the .357 Magnum Stevens had been wearing. His conclusion: The game warden had been killed with Stevens's gun. Then, as Craven related, "there was strong reaction from law enforcement personnel . . . they denied the report vehemently." Between five and ten thousand dollars was spent consulting out-of-state ballistics experts. A second test was conducted and Craven reversed his initial opinion. This time around, he said that the bullets had "probably" *not* been fired from Stevens's .357. It could have been passed off as an honest though costly mistake. But under cross-examination, the jury learned that Craven had been suspended from doing some criminological work since the incident, and that all of his other work was now subject to review. That, the defense suggested, smacked of pressure on Craven to tailor his opinion to the state's version of the Bull Camp murders. Craven had reversed himself once. Now Donnelly pressed him to re-reverse himself and incriminate Stevens, or at least Stevens's gun. The hapless criminologist refused, but Donnelly had scored a point anyway.

It was heavy, technical going, especially for those in the audience who had come for pure rodeo. It made the moments of comic relief all the more welcome. Chief among the amusements was George Nielsen's performance when he played fool to the audience with a grating, whiskey voice. "How many drinks did you have?" Donnelly asked him of the day of the murders. "Enough," responded Nielsen. "Enough to disorient you?" "I'm pretty hard to disorient, I'm not an alcoholic," he explained. Asked if fifteen drinks would seem an unreasonable daily average, the bar owner replied, "No, that would be easy." Unabashed, he claimed to drink twenty-five to thirty ounces of Bourbon a day. The audience loved his macho tomfoolery. Even Judge Lodge let loose a smile. When Nielsen likened his favorite drink, Early Times mixed with Seven-Up, to "a kid's milkshake," Dallas laughed out loud, too, and shook his head. The prisoner was frankly tickled also when a document examiner later analyzed the false signature he had used in South Dakota, pronouncing his unusual "e" and "a" as dead giveaways. But Dallas never mocked or guffawed. As if studying a river that needed fording, he quietly watched the passage of witnesses. In the audience, people were swayed by his calm. Terrible things were being said about him, but he seemed unperturbed, measured, sure of himself. "You could have counted the number of times he blinked," said John Accola of the *Idaho Statesman*. Maybe it was true then, maybe this donnish, even-tempered man whom George Nielsen had sworn "knew more than a father could teach a son," had been mightily provoked, backed into a corner. Juxtaposed to this unferocious, hardworking cowboy, the prosecution's "execution" charge seemed overblown. As the trial progressed, Donnelly and Mauk's crisp, natty oratory punched holes in a case everyone had thought was hermetically sealed. There had been enough recantations and contradictions among the state's witnesses, enough admissions of incomplete police work, and enough doubts wrenched from Stevens to make the jurors not just curious, but downright anxious to place their fingers in the wounds. And there was only one man, the defense attorneys had declared, who could lead them all through the valley of the shadow of death. On October 6, nearly a month into the trial, Claude Dallas took the stand.

He was relaxed and immediately engaging. Of his voice, which was hoarse, and the cough drops he chewed and sucked on throughout the day, the prisoner joked he was just "trying to catch" a cold. He had lost twenty or thirty pounds during his confinement, but looked fit all the same. From the moment he was sworn in, Claude Dallas was the finest witness the defense could have called upon, easygoing and succinct, helpful without surplus language. And such language, spiced everywhere with terms and words that were cogent but remote, a dialect that was somehow instantly familiar. There was no question about his spiritual origins. "I was interested," he explained, "in working the cow outfits, and wanted to get ahorseback." What exactly was this buckarooing?, his attorney asked. "Well, it's just . . . ," and Dallas paused to accumulate an answer, as if he had been asked what was air, what was water. "Buckarooing is just a man doing his job," he said, "working with livestock ahorseback, doing whatever work that has to be done on horseback regarding livestock and cattle, you know." Here was a physical man for whom the past was such a vital spark that he relinquished the buckarooing when he felt the buckarooing had relinquished its authenticity. "In my opinion," he stated, "the cow outfits were going to hell. I was interested in the old cow outfits and they had changed a lot in the last few years." For those who thought he had done nothing but cowboy and trap, his later vocations were nonetheless rugged and worthy: driving trucks, drilling water wells, setting barbwire fence, and working harvests on the hay and potato farms—wrestling the land. The modest narrative located him. It was like hearing Jack London read his résumé. Trucks and Blazers were "rigs";

to plow huge fields was to "rip a little ground." The col-loquialisms charmed, clearly speaking of a hard, dry haul through the high Sonoran desert, not merely for passage be-yond, not merely to rummage through quaint, frontier motifs, but to survive. He had abandoned himself to the heart of the Country, learning the lessons, poor but never starving. Nothing declared this faith in survival as distinctly as his taste for wild game. The thread tying together ten years of dusty living in the ION region was his trapping, and when he trapped, he ate meat. It wasn't hunting that he did—hunting sounded like rec-reation, when in fact the venison and wild horsemeat were daily necessities. What Dallas did was "knock down" meat ani-mals "to last me through the winter," dress them out, hang the quarters, and carve off steaks. Meat was his eucharist, it con-nected him to the land. "A man's got to eat," he enunciated for the court. "I mean you've got two things to eat, you either eat venison or you eat beef." (Or horsemeat, he added later.) As for eating cow, though, "I've never killed another man's beef. And I don't want anybody getting the idea I do." It was a small but breathtaking remark, brilliant with implication. He had poached and freely confessed it ("It's not something I'm ashamed of . . ."), but never had he rustled cows, never violated the western code.

His story built chronologically, unrelentingly mythical, a tale of trapping, buckarooing, and desert survival drenched with names such as Devil's Corral, Coyote Hole, the 45 Ranch, and, finally, Bull Camp. At long last, twenty-one months after breaking camp in the Owyhee gorge, the trapper connected his circle and, as the jury and audience listened, met again with the characters in his tragedy. There was Ed Carlin, the 45's leasee, "ahorseback." "I invited him up to camp for a bite to eat and a cup of tea . . . he didn't want anything to eat, so I built a fire and boiled some water and made some tea. And we had some things to talk about. . . . He made it fairly clear that they didn't appreciate my being in the area . . . that was their country. I told him that there had been no trapping in the country. I told him I'd looked for sign of trappers." Footprints, horse dung, tracks, browsed grass, feathers, fur, or any of a hundred other traces of life: These weren't signs, in the plural. They were altogether one and the same—sign. Plain, monosyllabic, mountain-man language. Sign. "I'd looked for sign of trappers. And hadn't found any old sets." And that, he left no doubt, constituted authority in the wilderness, the ability to read sign, to see truth. The ability to confront. "I noticed," said Dallas, "when I introduced myself, [Carlin] became very nervous . . . If I sat down, he sat down. If I stood up, he stood up. Every time I moved, he moved. He seemed very ill at ease." As the jury had already learned from Ed Carlin himself, Dallas had been wearing a gun on his hip. As with the poached venison, the trapper made no effort to hide the fact. "When I'm out, I always wear a revolver. Always." And as with the issue of poaching, he was glad to expound upon why. "I spend most of my time alone. I have no one to fall back on but myself. I've killed quite a bit of camp meat with them. I'm interested in firearms. I enjoy them. Also I've had some scrapes where I didn't have my handgun, and I'd like to have had one. I've been hung up several times alone. I had to cut myself away from a horse once . . . If I'm ever out away from camp and break a leg, I sure as hell want to have a gun with me." Guns and meat: the cowboy sacraments. He was modest, but certain. It was still the Country outback, a dangerous realm. The ancient vaqueros had known it was so. Dallas was only sharing a common wisdom.

Carlin rode off. Jim Stevens drove in. The trapper had cut sagebrush for firewood, grained his mules, and was checking his trapline when Stevens signaled from the rim with a gun-shot. They met on the trail. Already loaded with supplies, Stevens continued descending and Dallas continued up for a packload. "Just as I got over the rim, there was two men approaching me . . . and I saw what looked like a government rig behind them . . . They looked like Fish and Game. I noticed they were wearing—well, I noticed they had patches on, they had jackets on. One of them was wearing a hip gun." Immediately placing that gun as "a four-inch barrel Smith and Wesson revolver . . . looked like a stainless," Dallas met Bill Pogue and Conley Elms.

"I told [Pogue] that he was welcome in my camp," the prisoner related, "and that my camp was open. And I told him, I said, 'If you guys came out here a hundred and fifty miles just to give me a citation for meat, I can't see it.' And Pogue flew hot at that time. He seemed to be on the fight when he got out of the rig, as if he was primed. You know, he started off, he said, 'I'm going to tell you something right now, Dallas, if you want to get along with me.' And then he went into something. I don't recall the rest of it.

"I told him I had to hang meat up, you know, for subsistence. And I wasn't getting anywhere with him. He seemed to be getting hotter. And at that time, what was going through my mind was what in hell . . . you know, why was he so hot? I've never been approached like that."

The drama tightened fast, seldom interrupted by the defense attorney's questions. Dallas needed little prompting. He had an ingenious sense of pace and focus. The prosecutor objected several times that he was "engaging in narrative," but was overruled, and the hoarse voice spoke on, calm and earnest and soothed by cough drops. "At that time, I noticed that Pogue's hand, every time I moved or said something, Pogue's hand kept going to his gun." Like a practiced orator, Dallas injected Pogue's gun for the second time. Rhythmically, as if purposely to mesmerize his listeners, the prisoner subtly repeated that image over and over. "What I mean is there was nothing casual about the whole, I guess you would call it confrontation. They acted as if I had just robbed a bank. And I just couldn't understand all this. But I approached the back of Stevens's rig and started loading [my] pack. And when Pogue said something to Conley Elms . . . I saw Elms reach inside of his jacket . . . And I noticed then that he was wearing a shoulder rig and a gun." Asked about safety straps on the game wardens' holsters, Dallas remembered that Pogue's, at least, was off. "One of the first things that impressed itself upon my mind was that when Pogue got out of the rig, he was ready. You know, when his hand was on his gun, like I say, this was going through my mind, but I noticed that his weapon was clear. I mean it was in his holster, but it was ready." There it hung for the jury, cleared and sinister, a Sword of Damocles.

The three men prepared to descend to Bull Camp. While Dallas loaded groceries, Pogue fetched a small backpack, "one of those little kind of Boy Scout jobs, just a little cheap one," and a pair of handcuffs. "And I told him right then, you know, this thing had been—he'd been fairly hot with me and I just told him I thought he was a little bit out of line. Those [handcuffs] weren't necessary and they weren't needed. And he said something to me and then he told me I could go easy or I could go hard. Didn't make any difference to him." It became effectively a chant, "go easy or go hard," snaking sinuously through the tale alongside his key image, Pogue's gun. "Anytime I spoke to him or anytime I moved, he had his hand on the butt of his gun."

Flanked in front and off to one side, Dallas descended

toward the river with the two game wardens. Halfway down, he stopped for a breather. A brief exchange at that point was "short and not all that sweet. I just told Pogue, I said, 'You'll find traveling a lot easier on the trail.' And he just snapped something back to me about not to worry about them." Once in camp Dallas introduced Jim Stevens to Pogue. "I just thought I wasn't getting anywhere with the man [Pogue]; if I could get a conversation going between them, maybe things would cool off a little bit. I was somewhat bewildered at that time and somewhat apprehensive." It was victim language, a portrait of reason trying to comprehend outsized barbarians. Dallas depicted himself as a calm center around which other men stormed. In his presence, men like Ed Carlin blustered and were afraid, and men like Bill Pogue, "primed" and "on the fight," blustered and were fools. Authority was no cheap trifle, it was more than a patch you sewed on a shirt, more than handcuffs toted in a Boy Scout's daypack. You had to know yourself and know the land. Those were the square roots of power. And all Pogue seemed to know was the law: artificial seasons, quotas passed down by environmentalists, regulations that hammered honest men down and denied them honest meat.

Dallas and Stevens had been disarmed; at least, Pogue had emptied the obvious gun of each man. That still left Dallas with a .357 Magnum on his right hip, though. "I made no attempt to hide it," he said. "It made quite a bulge under my coat with the pack on . . . Pogue didn't say anything about the hip gun and I didn't say anything to him about it." In camp now, Dallas said, he tried to provide the ill-tempered game warden with a perspective. There were deer quarters hanging on every tent support, and it was not a promising dialogue. "We just went back and forth. I just explained the situation to him . . . that I had been there for a month . . . And that I thought it was unreasonable to give me a citation living under the conditions I was living under and the remote area I was living in." Pogue's response was blunt. He was going to search the tent. "I asked him if he had a search warrant. He said he didn't have a search warrant and he didn't need one . . . I told Pogue that tent was my home, that I didn't want him in it, and I believed he needed a search warrant . . . that went back and forth a little, and Pogue was getting loud and hot and he told me that I could go easy. He said, 'You can go easy or you can go hard, Dallas, it doesn't make any difference to me.'" And sliding alongside that chant was the gunslinger image. "I didn't know where this guy was coming from. I was a little worried about the gun deal at that time. It looked to me like he was itching to use it."

Elms untied the tent flaps, found the pelts, and emerged. The trapper tried again with Pogue, but the warden couldn't seem to hear reason. He stated, "We're going to confiscate those cats, Dallas." The trapper kept arguing. "I said at that point, 'Now wait a minute.' I said, 'You don't know that I didn't get those pelts in Nevada.' I said, 'I showed you my license . . .' I said, 'I'm running traplines here with some mules . . .' I told Pogue I was a hundred miles from town. I didn't have any transportation, that this was my home, this was where I lived, and any fur that I got in the area had to come back here. I said I didn't even know where the [state] line was. What was I supposed to do with any fur I got from Nevada, leave it hang on a bush down there?" Dallas tried every logic. Possibly, he conceded, he raised his voice. But "I was trying to stay under control." Pogue was like a deaf, evil spirit, though, destructive and menacing and implacable. The question of arrest or a mere citation came up. When Pogue stated he was going to arrest the trapper and take him in, Dallas asked for a citation for the

cats instead. The venison, though, was an issue of greater principle. Dallas would take a citation for the bobcats, but he continued arguing about the deer. It didn't work and the situation
took on added charge.

"Pogue was growing increasingly belligerent again, and
on the fight. And he told me I can go easy or I can go hard.
It didn't make any difference to him. And he told me he
was going to take me and the cats. And at that point I told
Pogue I couldn't go. I said, 'I've got my livestock, I've got my
mules here, and I've got all my equipment here.' And that I
can't leave them."

This time there was just one response. "He said, 'You can
go hard.'"

"What did you understand him to mean by that?" asked his
lawyer.

"Well, hard, that's only one way," explained Dallas. "That's
dead."

The eruption was close now. The audience well knew it.

"Well," said Dallas. "After that was said, you know, he said
to me, he said that to me, and he said he could carry me out.
And that's when Pogue, he was drawing his gun."

"He said he could carry you out?" his lawyer clarified.

"He did."

"Did he go for his gun at that point?"

"He did."

"Then what happened?"

"Well, I just reacted to it. I went for mine."

"Then what happened?" It was like a stop-action western,
an interview with Wyatt Earp after the OK Corral.

"Well, we fired."

"Did he fire at you?"

"He fired one round." Dallas took over in his hoarse voice.

"I fired, his gun went off, you know. And I fired again. And I spun [toward] Conley Elms, he was going for his gun. I fired one round at Elms, and Pogue was going down and bringing his gun to bear on me. It was up over the lower part of my body. I just threw two more shots at Pogue, and Elms was crouched, and I threw one at Elms. And I just ran back and into my tent and grabbed my twenty-two. It was inside of the tent and I ran out," he rasped, "and shot both men in the head. They were on the ground. Elms was face down and Pogue was on his back."

"Why did you shoot them in the head?"

"Well, I was a little bit out of my head at that stage. I was afraid. I was wound up . . . everything leading up to that had been so irrational, and I thought that the man was nuts. And I thought he was going to shoot me."

"Were you afraid?" the defense drummed.

"I would certainly say so." But even afraid, even a little bit out of his head with two men dead at his feet, Dallas still offered himself as the eye of the storm. Terrified, Stevens had rabbited upriver. With the rifle in his hands, Dallas stood there and watched the farmer stop and turn around and, like a supplicant, walk back to camp. "He came up to me and he was babbling something, almost incoherent . . . I asked him why he'd run off. He said, 'Because I was afraid you were going to shoot me.' I said, 'Jim, you should know better than that. I'd shoot myself first.'"

Thus Stevens then, and the jury and the audience now, came to understand that all was not chaos. The code still held. Here was a man who would not shoot another man's cow, who would shoot himself before he would shoot a friend. He comforted the shaken farmer. "I'm sorry I got you into this, Jim. I said the best thing you can do is go to your rig and head back to

Winnemucca and turn this deal in. The only thing I'll ask is that you take your time getting there." Almost penitent, the farmer refused, said Dallas. "He said, 'I don't want to do that, Claude. I'll help you anyway I can . . .' I told Jim right at that point, I didn't want those bodies in my camp. I told him I had to get those bodies out of here. I don't want those things in my camp."

By his account the afternoon was long and filled with drudgery. It differed here and there from Stevens's testimony, noticeably in remarks about self-defense that he claimed to have repeated, and by the perception that when they turned Elms's body over, a gun was lying free of its holster, proof that Dallas had faced annihilation. He didn't mention his observation about quartering Elms to get him up to the rim. His account took them to Paradise Hill, where Dallas again portrayed himself as cogent and orderly, surrounded by folk who were weaker, confused, and afraid. "George and Liz [Nielsen] and Jim were pretty much in a state of shock. At times when I spoke to them, it was like talking to a wall. I had to repeat myself. I mean that they were, at times, just out of it." There wasn't much more to be told, and so his lawyer had Dallas encapsulate the story again, from Pogue's first belligerence to his "easy or hard" threats and the hand peskily tagging his gun. Summarizing the ways he had tried to accommodate the menacing warden, Dallas concluded, "It was just, Christ, it was all that. When I told Pogue that, his immediate response was, you can go hard. And I told him right then, I said, 'You're out of line, Pogue, you're crazy. You can't shoot a man over a game violation.' And Pogue said, 'I'll carry you out,' and that's when I went for my gun. And I just, I did the only thing I felt I could've done to save my life." His attorney had no further questions.

The aim of course was to gut the prosecution's first-degree murder charge by portraying a lone, windswept trapper forced to defend himself against the long arm and heavy hands of lawmen. The language of the law was almost tailor-made to fit Dallas's self-defense plea, so parallel in wording and content that his performance on the stand showed its careful grooming. The definition of justifiable homicide in Idaho reads, "Where one, without fault is placed under circumstances sufficient to excite the fears of a reasonable man that another designs to commit a felony, or some great bodily injury upon him, and to afford grounds for reasonable belief that there is imminent danger of the accomplishment of his design, he may, acting under these fears alone, slay his assailant and be justified by the appearances. And as where the attack is sudden and the danger imminent, he may increase his peril by retreat; so situated, he may stand his ground, that, becoming his wall, and slay his aggressor, even if it be proved he might more easily have gained by flight." As Dallas had told it, a reasonable man had been afraid for his life, stood his ground, put his back against the wall, and slain his assailant. Pogue's quirky rage had served to highlight the trapper's reasonableness.

The prosecution had readied several ploys, among them the tried-and-true tactic of prodding this "reasonable" man into a display of unreasonable temper. But Dallas had more presence of mind than to bluster or argue. He was firm. When Clayton Anderson challenged him about remarks drawn from other witnesses' testimonies and attributed to Dallas, damning and telling statements such as "You're welcome in my camp, but leave your badge outside" or "This is Murder One for me," Dallas patiently explained that each was out of context or a misquote. And each time, the prisoner courteously offered to set the record straight. "I can tell you what I said," he volunteered.

# REWARD
## UP TO
# $20,000

For information leading to the Arrest and Conviction of
## CLAUDE LAFAYETTE DALLAS, JR.
for the Murder of two Idaho Fish and Game Officers on January 5, 1981.

- Date of Birth: 3-11-50
- Height: 5' 10''
- Weight: 180 lbs.
- Brown Hair (may be shoulder length)

- Brown Eyes
- May have full beard
- Wears glasses
- Social Security No. 270-49-0296

Subject is an accomplished trapper and shooter.

## SUBJECT IS ARMED AND EXTREMELY DANGEROUS.

CONTACT —
Sheriff Tim Nettleton, Owyhee County, Idaho - Murphy, Idaho 83650 — (208) 495-2441

The reward poster

Various lawmen warm themselves on the rim above Bull Camp several days after the murders.

An Army National Guard helicopter delivers more investigators on the desert.

The body of Bill Pogue was still missing when Idaho Fish and Game officers gathered for a memorial service.

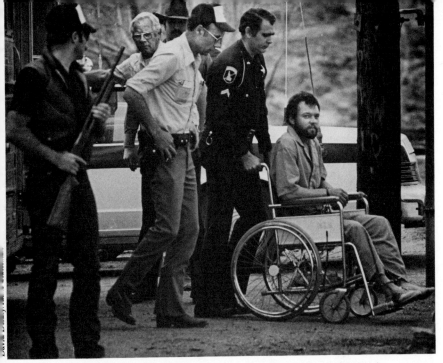

Shackled, bellycuffed and under heavy guard, Dallas is transported into the Murphy jail in the Owyhee Desert.

Twenty months after the murders, Humboldt County Sheriff Frank Weston (*left*) and his investigator Stan Rorex discover the remains of Bill Pogue.

After the trial, Owyhee County Sheriff Tim Nettleton greets Dee Pogue, the widow of his old friend Bill Pogue.

With Hoyt Wilson, the rancher who gave a teenage dreamer his first chance to cowboy, Dallas arrives at the courthouse to receive his sentence.

Asked why he couldn't bring in his meat like anyone else, why in short he felt above the law and exceptional, his answer was unabashed. "Not anyone else that I know lives like I do or under the conditions that I do . . . You can't bring in cut meat and frozen meat. Meat has to be hung in carcass form to keep."

"You could have made arrangements," pressed Clayton Anderson.

"I could have made arrangements," Dallas shot back, "but even if I'd wanted to, I couldn't have afforded it." He hadn't budged for Ed Carlin or Bill Pogue. He didn't budge for Clayton Anderson. When the prosecutor called his gunstocks "combat" grips, Dallas corrected him—"custom" grips. He knew the power of words, and also their slipperiness. "I would have took 'em on the rim, but they would have killed me up there" (Stevens's version) became "if they had taken me on the rim, they would have killed me."

The prosecution had one tangible proof that the murders had been premeditated, evidence suggesting a long history of his being antiauthoritarian. They had been restricted from bringing Dallas's previous arrest for draft evasion into the trial, but they saw two of Dallas's books, *No Second Place Winner* and *Kill or Get Killed*, as revealing that he had trained for just such a fast-draw gunbattle. Carefully Anderson set up his ambush, establishing that Dallas had known his poaching was illegal, that he had been forewarned that game wardens might visit, and that logically they would cite or arrest him. The trapper acknowledged each assertion. Foreknowledge in place, Anderson requested that the bailiff bring forward the evidence. In midsentence, before Anderson's request was half out of his mouth, the defense interrupted.

The jury was removed while Dallas's lawyers argued that

the books would prejudice opinion. The judge agreed. It was a major defeat. The defense objected, too, when Dallas was handed a lever action rifle similar to his .22 trap gun, and Anderson attempted to replay the coups de grâce with himself as victim. The objection was sustained.

The center of gravity had shifted. Frustrated, Anderson asked why Dallas hadn't simply surrendered early on. Citing "the lynch-mob attitude that the state tried to cultivate," the prisoner said, "I think it would have been suicide if I had been picked up there. And I believed it then and I believe it now even more so."

It was not a perfect performance—the sole remorse he expressed was for having touched the bodies—but his belief in the rightness of his way resounded with conviction. He had broken some game laws, true, but the real violations had been committed against him. His home had been invaded, his lifestyle ignored. A choleric lawman had driven a hundred miles into the desert to disarm and threaten him. "All I wanted to do was keep those men from killing me," he concluded. "I responded in the only way I could have to have prevented those men from killing me." He was a reasonable man, so reasonable that in the final hours of his testimony he even gave back the body of Bill Pogue. It was to be the prosecution's only real accomplishment all day.

With the dead man in the bed of George Nielsen's truck, Dallas narrated, he had driven off into the night. It was foggy and he had become disoriented. "I didn't know where I was going. I just wanted to get rid of the body. I couldn't think of any place to put it. I wasn't sure of my bearings. I figured I had to get off the road. I pulled into the brush. That's where I buried Bill Pogue."

"Could you trace your route of travel on a map?" Anderson asked.

"Certainly," Dallas complied. "Quite easily, I'm sure." He was altogether willing to help, as if this were a matter they had somehow neglected to clear up earlier. "I'm really not sure where the fence is," he pondered. "I could tell you where it is."

"If you could just give us an approximate location on the map."

"I would be happy to," said Dallas. "Would you like me to mark the location of Bill Pogue's body?" Reporters had begun streaming for the door and telephones. In their midst was Sheriff Nettleton.

It was late afternoon by the time Frank Weston, Stan Rorex, and Dan Nielsen (no relation to George), a reporter for the *Humboldt Sun* arrived on the far side of Sand Pass Road. A hundred searchers had swept this area months before, with no result. "It was right where he said it was," Weston said. "It didn't take us two minutes to find it. We followed the directions, got out of our vehicle, and walked right up to it." Vertebrae and rib bones lay scattered in the dust around a shallow indentation. "Save it," Rorex advised. "We'll back down the road a ways and make it a crime scene." As they backed out slowly, Weston saw a patch of green among the sagebrush. "We got out," said Rorex, "and there was some green Levi on the ground, and in the Levi was a thighbone. That was it." The sheriff and his deputy didn't dare dig for more, not without observing procedure. It was too late to begin work that day. The site had become public information, however, and an Idaho news helicopter was already en route. "And so I left Dan there with a vehicle, a radio, and a shotgun," said Rorex. "I told him to keep people out, even if he had to stick the shotgun in their face and keep them out."

In the morning they returned to the base of the Bloody Runs with a team, sectioned the area by grid, and began the search. The indentation which they had presumed to be the grave quickly turned out to be a false start. As Dallas had twenty-one months earlier, they hit rock just a few inches down. Over by the pants leg, though, the dirt was softer. Digging, sorting, and sifting dirt through a mesh, they found the leg bones still in a pair of boots and a skull with a small-caliber bullet hole above the left ear. "The midsection was all gone," said Rorex. "Dallas had trapped all through that area. He knew exactly where he was. I imagine that he knew there was coyote den there, he knew where it was and it wasn't difficult to dig out. Once we dug the body out, I found a hole that led out and vertebrae in the hole. He'd buried the body and the coyotes had come in the hole and couldn't find their den, but they found the body and started eating on it that way and then dug it out from the top." Not unexpectedly, the small daypack containing the wardens' service badges, pieces of their clothing, and, most significantly, the gun Pogue had supposedly fired at Dallas were never found. Beyond recalling where the body was located, Dallas's mind had gone conveniently blank.

A local mortuary received the remains, and next day the game warden was returned to the state of Idaho. Pogue did not rest in peace though, not yet. Even as the dust was being brushed from his bones, he was standing trial. At the start of the proceedings, Judge Lodge had ruled out all evidence and testimony regarding Pogue's character. "The law is clear," he had said, "that specific acts of violence by deceased individuals are inadmissible, particularly when the defendant was unaware of previous acts." But in the face of defense protests, Lodge eventually relented. The old tales of Pogue's manner were trotted out. No sooner was the defense team given access to Pogue's personnel file, than they charged it had been censored, with all negative material or complaints edited out. The prosecution denied it.

Laverne Inzer, the circuit-riding preacher, took the stand and tried to tell his outrageous tale about gunplay with two men of the cloth, but it was stricken from the record because the judge had limited testimony to events within the past five years. Inzer stubbornly complained, "It's not often that I get a gun pulled on me," and that, too, was stricken from the record. Danny Martinez, a dashing thirty-three-year-old Paradise horse trader, auctioneer, brander, roper, Golden Gloves boxer, and friend to Dallas, given to wearing black hats and driving black pickups, took the stand. Asked why he had identified himself as Dallas's adopted brother on a visit to the Canyon County jail, Martinez explained that only family members had been admitted to the jail, and besides they were like brothers anyway, because Liz Nielsen had been like a mother to them both. With respect to Pogue, the defense asked him, how did people on the range characterize the warden "in terms of dangerousness, violence, turbulence, and aggression"? Taking his cue, Martinez embraced the whole slew of terms and answered, "Every one of them." The prosecution managed to extract from Martinez that Pogue's bad reputation had begun after he was killed at Bull Camp. Next to the flood of accusations, that addendum seemed a very minor point, though.

A Boise electrician took the stand and testified that Pogue had been "extremely hostile, extremely belligerent" in his hunting camp several years before. "His attitude was rude and abusive. He acted like we had committed a major crime." In response, the prosecution produced the game warden who had actually cited the electrician on that day. Bill Pogue had been nowhere present.

To belie the claims of nineteen character witnesses describing Pogue as a bully, the prosecution produced its own witnesses, among them a former Idaho City mayor and trapper

named Roger Jackson. Jackson had dealt regularly with the
game warden, only once in two hundred times butting heads
with him. But on that one occasion he had threatened to shoot
Pogue. "He thought we were trapping mink and said he was
going to search my vehicle," said Jackson. "I told him he needed
a search warrant and he told me he didn't need one. He started
to reach for the door and I told him I'd shoot him. He got a
funny look on his face and said, 'I don't think you have anything.'" Jackson had been called to the stand to rebut the portrait of a bully; inadvertently he contributed to it. There had
been enough backfires that it was not remarkable that the defense team, bolstered by Dallas's firm, confident confession,
had lifted the simplistic "protrait of evil" from the trapper and
bestowed it upon his Bull Camp enemy.

　　"We assumed that the defense attorneys would try to dis-
credit the officers," said Dee Pogue, "but I was really horrified
to find that . . . Claude Dallas was a spectator in the courtroom
and it was Bill who was on trial." For the Pogues it was a
special bitterness. Not only had Dallas stolen from them a father and husband and brother, and furthermore set him up as
an enemy of the public, he had also cheated his victim of the
resting place he would have wanted. "Every time I drove over
Horseshoe Bend and into Boise," said Steve Pogue, "I could see
the Owyhee Mountains over there and I'd always get an empty
feeling in my belly because I didn't know where my dad was."
Now, at least, they knew. The game warden's remains were
cremated, and because, in Steve's words, "he'd rather be under
that sagebrush [by the Bloody Runs] like he was than in some
cemetery plot in Boise," the family scattered the ashes. But the
Bull Camp violence had poisoned Pogue's cherished desert,
and they couldn't bring themselves to commit the ashes to the
Owyhee. Instead, the ashes were scattered by plane over the

rugged Sawtooth wilderness in central Idaho. In that sense Dallas had defeated the game warden three times, once in battle, a second time by banishing his remains from the Owyhee Desert, and a third time in court by reversing the portrait of evil. How effective that reversal was, only the jury could finally signify. For nearly a month they had listened to the witnesses, mutely studying the tears, accusations, antics, and stratagems. Now it was their turn to speak. On October 13 the attorneys concluded their cases. Judge Lodge issued instructions to the twelve jurors, and the panel was sequestered to make their verdict.

If the jury returned swiftly, courtroom pundits observed, then justice belonged to the rope. If not, Dallas might live. At the trial's outset, there had been no doubt how the jury would swing. By the sixth day of deliberation, there was nothing but doubt. The jury was at a stalemate. Jurors were having to be walked separately around the courthouse to cool off. Several times, crying, they had asked for further instructions from the judge.

On day one, Milo Moore, a forty-five-year-old grocer was elected foreman, in part because it was felt a man's voice could overpower the inevitable arguments better than a woman's. After reading the judge's instructions, each juror was given time to express her or his feelings and thoughts about the case. "Everybody wanted to talk at once," said Marlys Blickenstaff. "It all spilled out." When someone opined that Dallas had finished off the wardens like trapped game, Jimmie Hurley, a writer in charge of public relations for the Snake River Stampede Rodeo, broke into tears. "But this isn't animals," she cried. "These are human beings." That marked the beginning of what other jurors considered by day five to be their greatest obstacle, Hurley's subjectivity. "She kept bringing up feelings," said

Blickenstaff. "She was [arguing with] total and irrational emotion," agreed Donna Diehl, a sales clerk. "She was saying if we
let him go free, he'd go to Alaska and kill people. Those poor
grandkids [of Pogue] would never know their grandparents.
She could never, ever believe any word Dallas said."

What Dallas had said became important. Comparing their
notes on the testimonies of Stevens and Dallas, the majority of
jurors agreed that the farmer's uncertainty had reduced his
story to the same reliability as Dallas's. Hurley was adamant,
however, that Dallas was a liar. "I reasoned with them," she
said, "that I would tend to believe Stevens . . . based on the fact
of who had the most to lose. I said to them, Dallas admitted he
tried to fabricate a story to protect Stevens. Why would he not
be more likely to fabricate one to protect himself?" Her
obstinacy, the others felt, was dogmatic. "I guess a person
standing up for conviction is a courageous thing," said Sheilda
Talich, another juror. "But only to a point. When their convictions are not based on facts that the law will allow us to take, it
ceases to be courageous and becomes an injustice." Though
Jimmie Hurley was not the sole obstacle to a verdict, she was
the most vocal. Whether or not Hurley was completely respon-
sible, mention of Dallas's arrest for draft evasion was attributed
to her. It had appeared in the press but not in testimony, and
so was extraneous information barred from consideration. Hurley was asked if she could disregard it, and replied, yes, she
could. That was not good enough. On the sixth day, Judge
Lodge received a note from the deadlocked jury describing
Hurley's prejudice.

After a grueling month of testimony and consideration and
over one hundred thousand dollars in expenses, it appeared
that Lodge had a hung jury on his hands. By this time, the
prosecution was morose. "As the jury stayed out longer and

longer," said Jerry Conley, the Fish and Game Director, "we became less surprised." Anticipating the worst, Clayton Anderson twice requested that a mistrial be declared. Sensing their advantage, the defense attorneys and Dallas himself argued against a mistrial. "It astounds one to think that the prosecutor in this case, who has spent two years accumulating evidence and one month at trial—at considerable expense to Owyhee and Canyon counties—now wants to declare a mistrial and proceed against Mr. Dallas," declared Bill Mauk. The judge dismissed Hurley, which left the jury with only eleven members. Idaho state law was unclear about whether an eleven-member jury would be constitutional; despite this Dallas optimistically waived his right to a complete panel. "I would like to continue with an eleven-member jury regardless of the outcome," he told the judge.

In an effort to save the trial, Lodge appointed an alternate juror. Two subjurors had attended the entire trial in the event someone took ill or an emergency called them away. Using an alternate to revitalize a hung jury was unusual, but there seemed to be no other option. Joyce Blanksma, therefore, took Hurley's place in the jury room. There remained some concern that Blanksma, who had not been sequestered with the others during deliberation, might have been influenced by media accounts by this time. The risk was weighed and accepted. "Start deliberating again from the beginning," Lodge ordered the reconstructed jury. "[Set] aside your earlier deliberations as though they never occurred."

The new juror was given a crash course in the deliberations. She studied the instructions and listened to evidence for both sides. "We had not reached a final agreement at all," said Sheilda Talich, "and so we completely started over. And I think it made it easier for us to explain why we had come to the decision [each] arrived at." The jurors spent one final night at the Sundowner Motel. Next day, just after their lunch was delivered, a unanimous verdict was reached. Outside the jury room, reporters could hear their cheers and clapping. Dallas was led into the court. The jurors filed in. The verdict was read.

He was guilty, not of first- or second-degree murder, but of two counts of voluntary manslaughter . . . "the unlawful killing of a human being without malice—upon a sudden quarrel or heat of passion." "We just figured Pogue drew his gun and Dallas was a better marksman, that he was put in a position of self-defense," jury foreman Moore explained later. "Dallas was a faster draw. He won out." If only Dallas had refrained from grabbing his trap rifle and shooting each warden in the head, Moore amplified, the trapper would have been acquitted altogether. The head shots, though, had exceeded his claim of justifiable homicide.

On the two counts of using a firearm to commit a crime, he was found guilty. He was guilty, too, of concealing evidence, but was acquitted of resisting arrest. In all, Dallas now faced a possible sentence of fifty years and six months. The judge set the sentencing date at December 1.

It was a verdict neither side wanted to hear, and cast the whole issue into a sort of limbo. Given his growing popularity with the audience and the jury's extended debate, Dallas had begun to expect he might walk free. He was noticeably dejected, and his lawyers filed for acquittal along with a motion requesting bail. The prosecution, lawmen, and the victims' families were stunned and furious. "He lied on the witness stand," Clayton Anderson charged. "The Claude Dallas who was in the courtroom and the Claude Dallas [at Bull Camp] are two different individuals. I think the jurors believed who they saw and heard on the witness stand. No one will be able to convince me otherwise. This is a verdict the jury will have to live with." And then, in his own defense, he added, "There isn't anything the state could have done in the case that we could have done better." The Fish and Game Department was outraged, claiming that the verdict had "cheapened and jeopardized the lives of all police officers." The director, Jerry Conley, stated that "the jury has told us that . . . enforcement of game laws is meaningless and that the lives of our Fish and Game officers or other law enforcement officers are expendable—or at least that the last man alive is telling the truth." Characteristically blunt, Ed Pogue put it more plainly. "It's open season on game wardens," he warned. "If you don't want a hundred-dollar ticket you just have to put a hole in [the game warden]." Immediately after the verdict, Eddie Pogue announced his intention of suing Dallas. Calling the jury's decision the "damnedest injustice I've ever encountered or heard of" and "a hell of a miscarriage of justice," Pogue went on to say, "If you want justice in this country, you have to do it yourself. I said [Dallas] won't be allowed to get away with it, and he won't."

In short, the legend was unfinished. No one but the jurors felt justice had been served. A television news station furnished a phone number for those interested in registering their opinion, called the results a survey, and announced that an overwhelming number felt Dallas deserved worse. In effect a pseudo-lynch mob electronically hanged the prisoner. "I live in backwards country," Dallas's father later complained. "This South Carolina is not known to be an intellectual haven. The blacks down here get shitty treatment. But they don't get anything as bad as that deal out there." He wrote a letter to the *Idaho Statesman* condemning the "Pogues of this world" as "evil men, who themselves are criminals, have used the law to bring righteous men death or imprisonment since the beginning. Any man who uses the Court to destroy his fellow man commits treason against the State and destroys all that should be held sacrosanct." For all the thundering and anger in Idaho, however, there was still hope in both camps that the judge would be extreme at his sentencing. The prosecution wanted all fifty years for the killer. Dallas, knowing "damn well" he wouldn't get off scot-free, was expecting two or three years at the most. That sense of optimism was buttressed when, to lawmen's utter disbelief, a one-hundred-thousand-dollar bail was posted. Dallas had been in jail for six months. Now he was free to wander through the three states that joined in the Owyhee. It was to the old ION stomping grounds that he returned now until sentencing, which was reset for January 5, 1983.

During part of that period, he was with a woman. Some of the time he spent touring among the cowboys, horsebreakers, and mustangers he called friends in Paradise and elsewhere, roping and branding a bit, telling stories of his fugitive days, and how it was to be famous. *Rolling Stone* ran a laudatory piece on him in early December, and the overall vision of himself pitted against the law suited him fine. And then one morning he took a rifle and disappeared into the mountains of his early fantasy, the Steens Range above the Mann and Alvord ranches in Oregon. Here, an Ohio teenager had forged himself into a bygone cowboy, riding one, packing one, knocking down venison when he needed meat, contesting the land, and living with it. In that spirit, or as a gesture of defiance, or both, he stalked a bighorn ram and killed it. It was a senseless, highly personal hunt. Perhaps someone had mentioned during the trial that Pogue had loved bighorns. In any case, Dallas descended to the Mann Ranch with the poached carcass, where it was kept a close, though distasteful secret.

On the morning of January 5, 1983, black ice sheathed roads and highways throughout lower Idaho. South of Caldwell, patches of fog hung over the Owyhee Desert, much as it had on the day of the murders. Hoyt Wilson had volunteered to drive Dallas to the courthouse for sentencing. Along with Wilson's remarried mother, Coco Ickes (who had provided a portion of the bail), they ate breakfast together. "You don't mind if I don't go today, do you?" asked Ickes. "I really don't want to be there." Dallas looked up from his plate, thought about it, and said, "You know, I really don't want to be there either."

Despite predictions that he would vanish once released on bond, Dallas appeared at the courthouse on time. He was barbered, with the tails of a blue bandanna draped at the throat of his western-cut shirt. Except for a tractor cap, he was the buckaroo and trapper of old, from boots to sheepskin coat. He entered the courtroom, which was packed with spectators. They were there to see and hear how the moral was resolved, though outlaw myths never do the resolving. Character witnesses and law officers were given a last chance to influence the harshness of the sentence. Finally it was the judge's turn to speak.

"My heart is saddened by the series of human tragedies that occurred," he began. "Two families lost their loved ones. The person who probably loved freedom more than most of us because of his life-style, lost or forfeited his right to freedom." Lodge criticized those who had threatened jurors and himself (his dogs had been poisoned during the trial), and those who had damned the adversary system of justice. The media, particularly the television news polls, he said, had "advocated a state of emotional hypocrisy . . . you cannot try a person by public opinion." And then he declared, "Mr. Dallas, I can consciously tell you, sincerely tell you, that I do not believe the issue of self-defense arose at Bull Camp. By saying that, I do not mean by any stretch of the imagination that you are a bad person. The evidence is to the contrary . . . But I do not believe the issue of self-defense arose at Bull Camp." He listed his reasons, and then compressed them into one observation: "Your actions were motivated by your desire to ensure your own freedom as opposed to an actual threat of life or limb." At last he passed sentence. Dallas was to serve two consecutive terms of ten years each for the shootings, plus another ten years for having used a firearm in the crime, and six months for concealing evidence. Thirty years was the maximum sentence he would impose, and he kept it indeterminate. "I am putting you in a position to prove to society that you are the type of person you say you are." Providing he was a model prisoner, Dallas would be eligible for parole in seven to ten years, though the judge warned him that public sentiment was against an early parole.

With that, Dallas was led away. Next morning, two years to the day after Bull Camp, Sheriff Nettleton drove Dallas to the Idaho State Penitentiary outside Boise. The prisoner said nothing. His hair and beard were shorn away, and he was given a pair of rough white cotton overalls.

Lawmen, still grumbling about the topsy-turvy verdict, felt partially vindicated by the sentence. Claude Dallas, Sr., on the other hand, was outraged. He laid blame everywhere . . . with the jury, the judge, Fish and Game, Nettleton ("a ragass" with "family roots everywhere in that county . . . ought to chop some of them off"), even the lawyer who had made such a remarkable defense ("He's a damned junkie . . . overdosed right after the trial and they disbarred him"). In another of his fiery letters to the *Idaho Statesman,* he lectured that society was unsafe so long as "a man's name and liberty can be taken away upon the testimony of rogues, informants and detectives. Add to this a tyrannical judge and nefarious lawmen, and you have a tyrannous court." No one was surprised when the case was appealed to the state supreme court, nor that Lodge refused to release Dallas on bail during the long appeals process.

"Knowing the kind of person Claude Dallas is," Clayton Anderson remarked after the sentencing, "ten years in prison for Dallas would be like life for anyone else." Prison . . . the joint . . . became a somber, slow epilogue to the legend. Out of sight, he languished, not just a prisoner, but *the* prisoner, the outlaw cowboy with silence for an archangel. Though he granted interviews to no one, his picture and story kept appearing in magazines, newspapers, and books. A local singer cut a 45-rpm record entitled "The Ballad of Claude Dallas" ("Game man, what have I done?/ Game man, don't pull that gun"). The prisoner refused to autograph or even acknowledge the tribute. He just wanted the world to forget about him so he could get on with his life. But even behind bars, celebrity was inescapable.

He was greeted as a hero by the other inmates and accorded what passes for spoils in any prison: a good job, new clothing, respect. His adoption by a so-called Mexican Mafia provided him a modicum of safety from violence, though not from harassment by the prison staff and at least one opportunistic stoolie. Upon learning that Dallas had somehow gained garden privileges and a cherished job in the auto shop, the warden promptly revoked them. "That broke Claude's heart to lose that garden," said his father. "It was in shape and the melons were ready to pick." Tardy by fifteen minutes one afternoon, he was reportedly thrown in the hole. In October 1983, an inmate supposedly approached the warden, contending that Dallas was having a gun smuggled into prison for an upcoming breakout. Some sort of proof was required, which the inmate arranged . . . a bit too transparently. Wire cutters were found in Dallas's gym locker, but it turned out the locker had been used by the stoolie immediately beforehand. He tried again. Two days later the inmate visited Dallas in his cell and used his trash can for a seat. An hour later guards checked the cell and found a set of lock picks in Dallas's trash. It was enough to remand Dallas to closed custody. "They ride hell out of him," his father railed. "The guards were issued full-size posters of Claude to practice with. But Claude don't care. He said to hell with them. And I feel the same way. I'm an old man, but if I could buck Claude side by side, I'd like to face them all, damn it. I'd go down with him. You can't die but once, if you fight. You die a thousand times if you don't."

Whether or not life-size posters of Dallas were actually printed for target practice (and the rumor seems to have begun with a local television station), the story fit the mold of a warrior in chains. That he had enemies who wore uniforms and abused their powers kept him viable, lending dimension to an otherwise tedious fate. "Oh, he's toed the line and all that," a friend assured. "But if he ever gets a clear shot at the wall, he's gone, there's no doubt in my mind." In Paradise and the ION region, jailhouse clichés cropped up like cheatgrass, with people swearing that the guards practically invite prisoners to escape, just to chase, catch, and kill them. "If he escapes," said Coco Ickes, "he'll either get away or he'll be killed, because he'll never be captured again." Among those watching expectantly for the break for freedom is Eddie Pogue. "I'm not making any threats," he said. "But I've got an idea Dallas will get his in the end. I haven't seen justice satisfied. The son of a bitch is a cold-blooded murderer. He should've been hung." Parole or escape, either way, Pogue promised, "the son of a bitch is going to have to sleep with both eyes open. I think he knows that."

★   ★   ★

South and west from Boise, like a wall distinctly shielding the city from its origins, hang the Owyhee Mountains, just barely visible from the prison. On their far side the desert sprawls, a magnet, folk insist, that tugs at Claude Dallas minute by slow minute. Someday he will return. Perhaps the Mexican Mafia will catapult their shining vaquero toward his memory of frontier, the Country where men still hang meat up, and winter is a vast monastery rich with emptiness and fabulous creatures . . . mustangs, rattlesnakes, coyotes, and cougars. Or he'll see a low wall or an open door. One slight chance, they say, Claude will do the rest. Maybe he'll even surprise them all and serve his time. However he returns, no one can imagine him free for long without a gun. Avengers will stalk him. Blood will feed the land. Out there, the legend goes, a life seized from fiction will end. They want him loose, some to stake the trapper down tight to the earth once and for all, others to season their sunsets and sage rites. It's all the same. The sun gleams bright on Owyhee cattle. The gorges are cool and repetitious. Scarce water keeps on carving the walls of the labyrinth deeper.